Spot the Difference Oute

A Fun Search and Find Books for Children 6-10 years old

by Nick Marshall

Find 5 Differences in Each Puzzles

Can you find them all?

Copyright © 2021 by Nick Marshall. All rights reserved.
No part of this book may be reproduced in any form or by any electronic or mechanical means, including information storage and retrieval systems, without written permission from the author, except for the use of brief quotations in a book review.

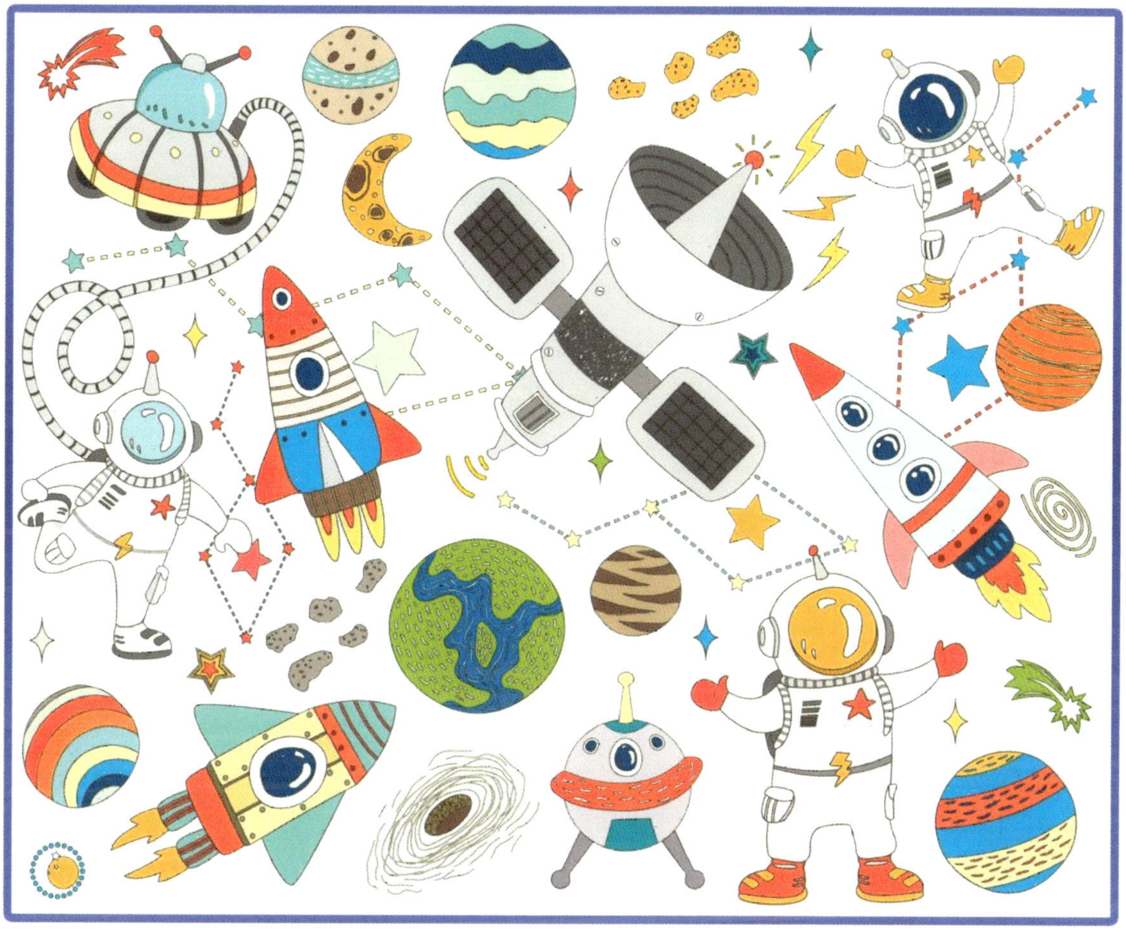

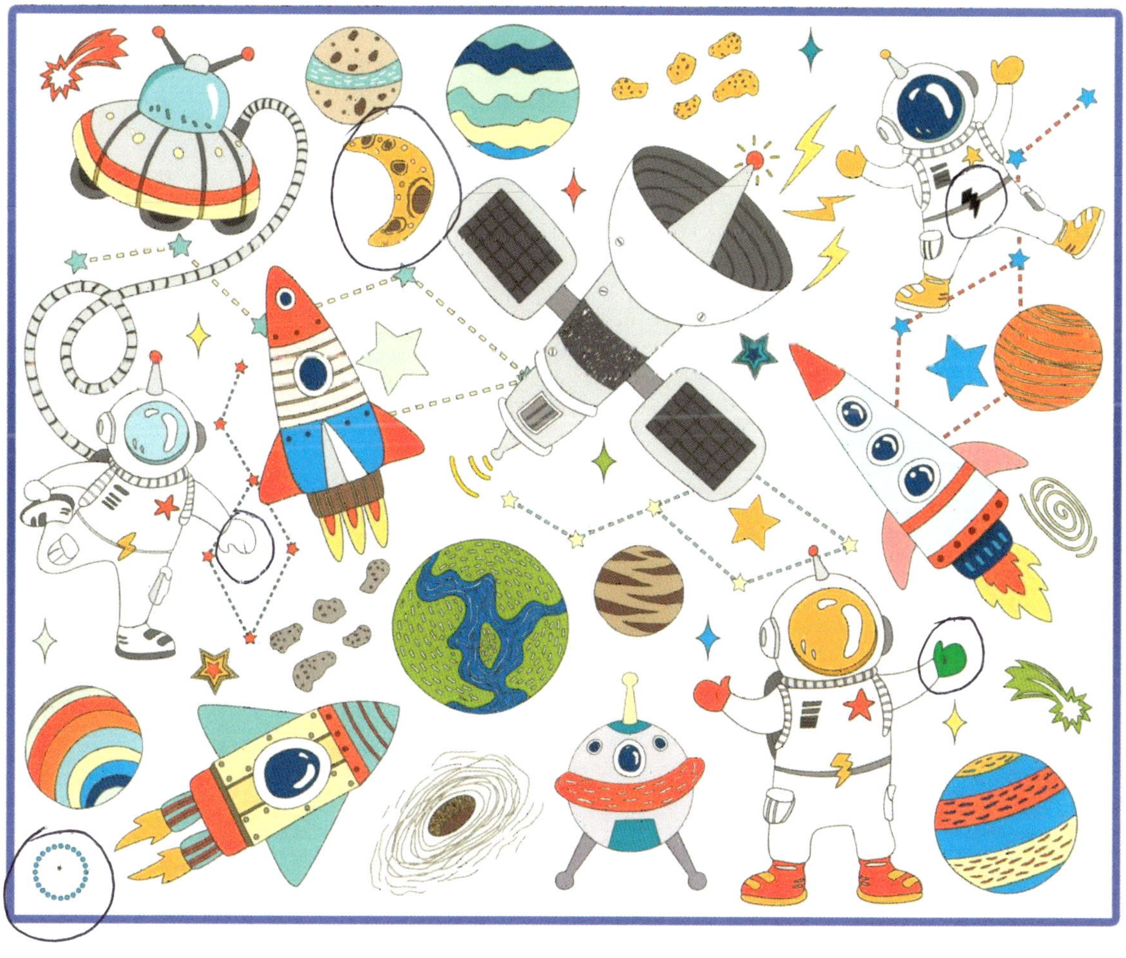

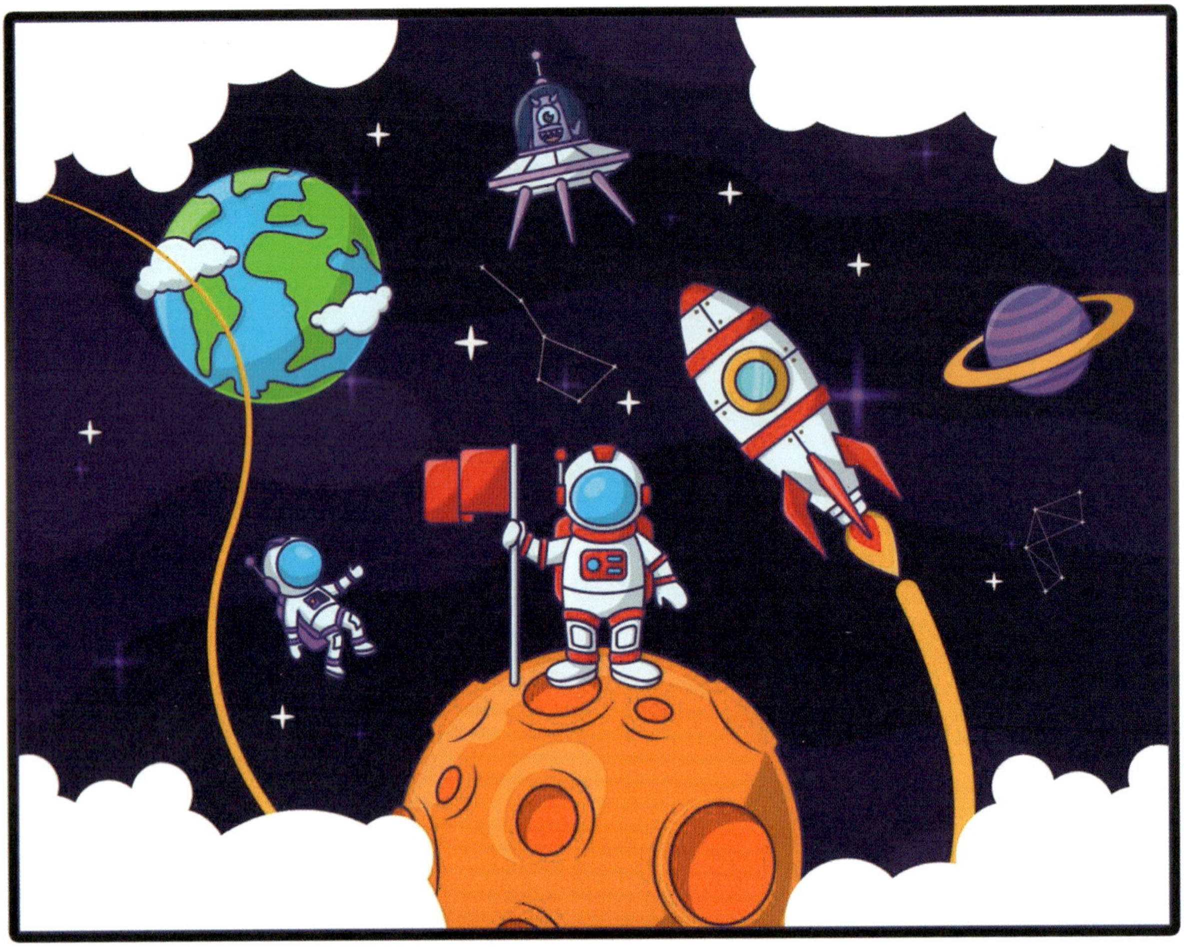

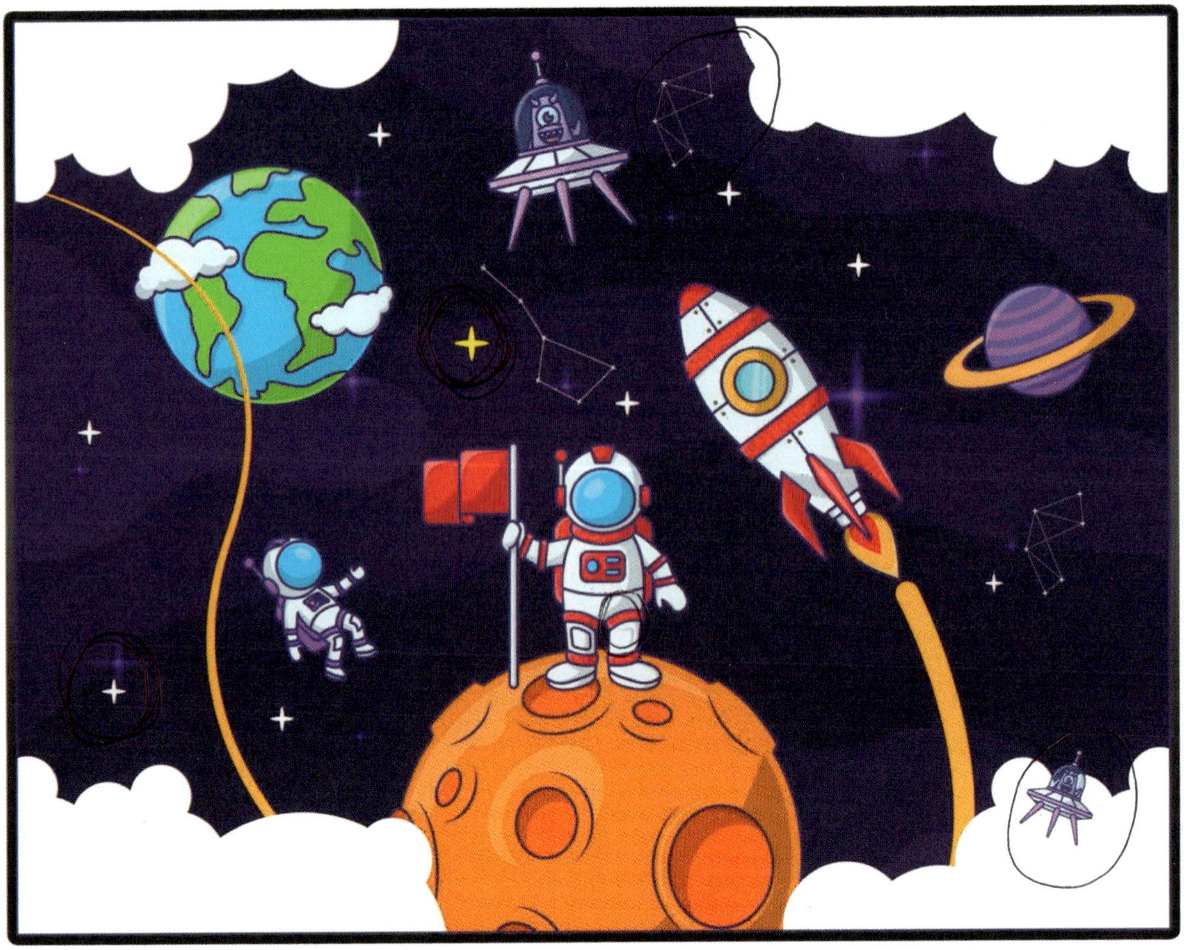

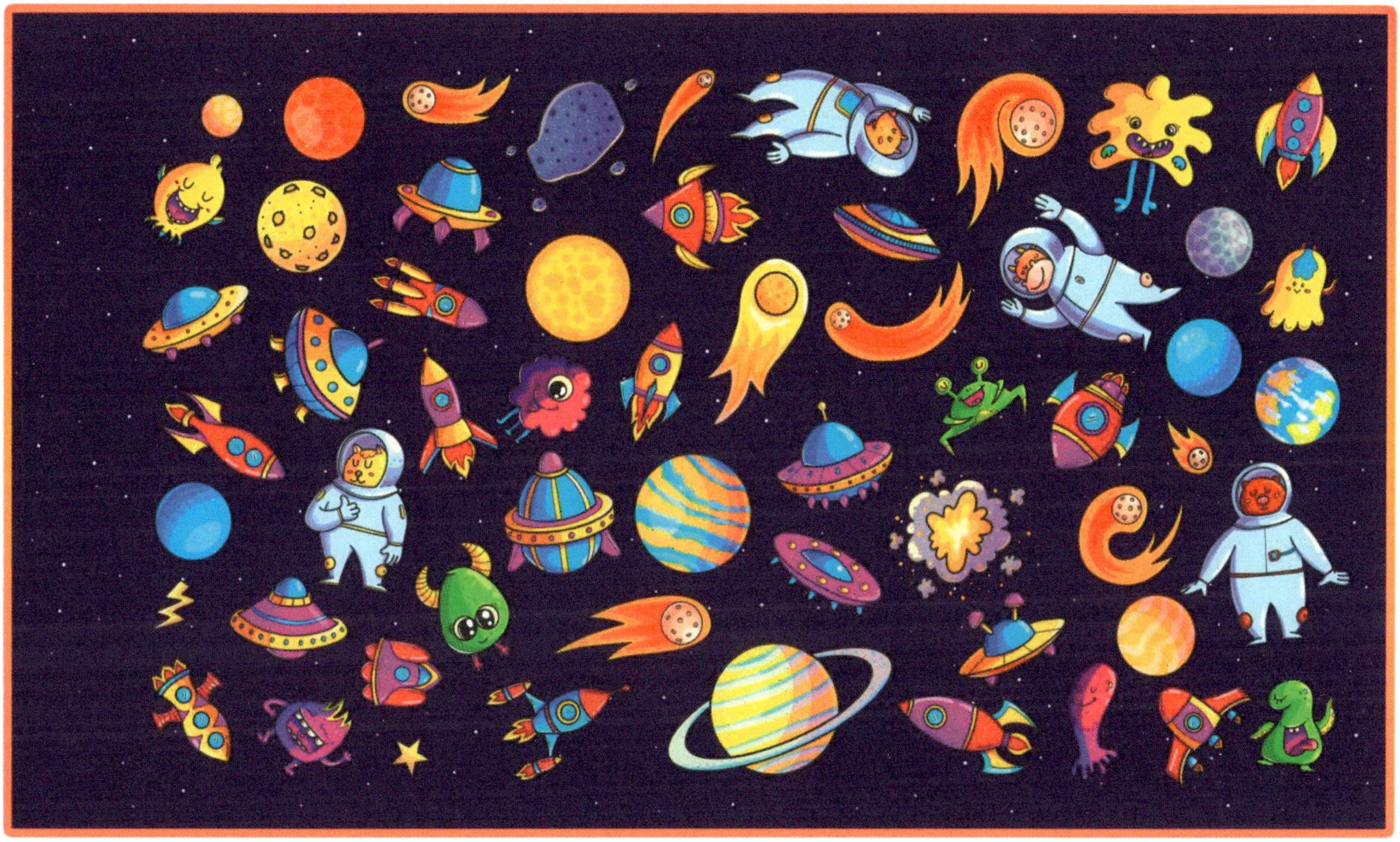

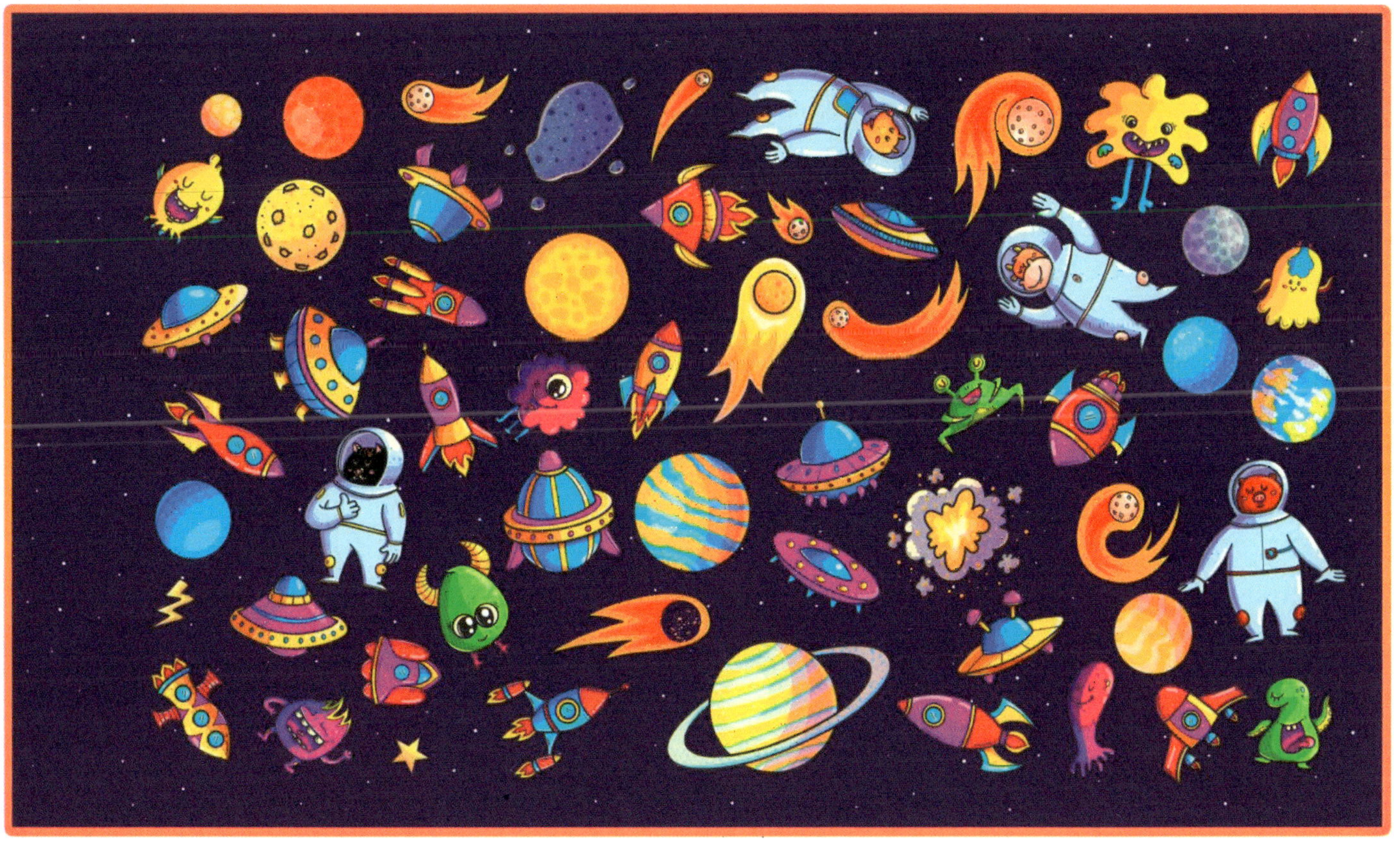

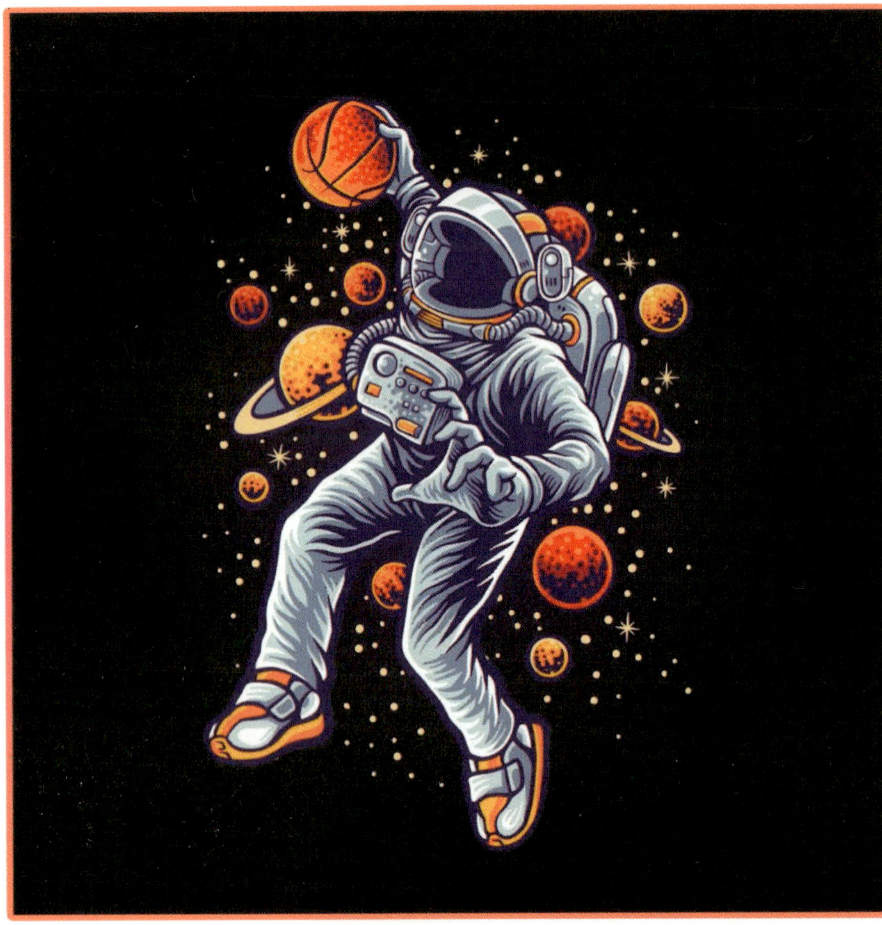

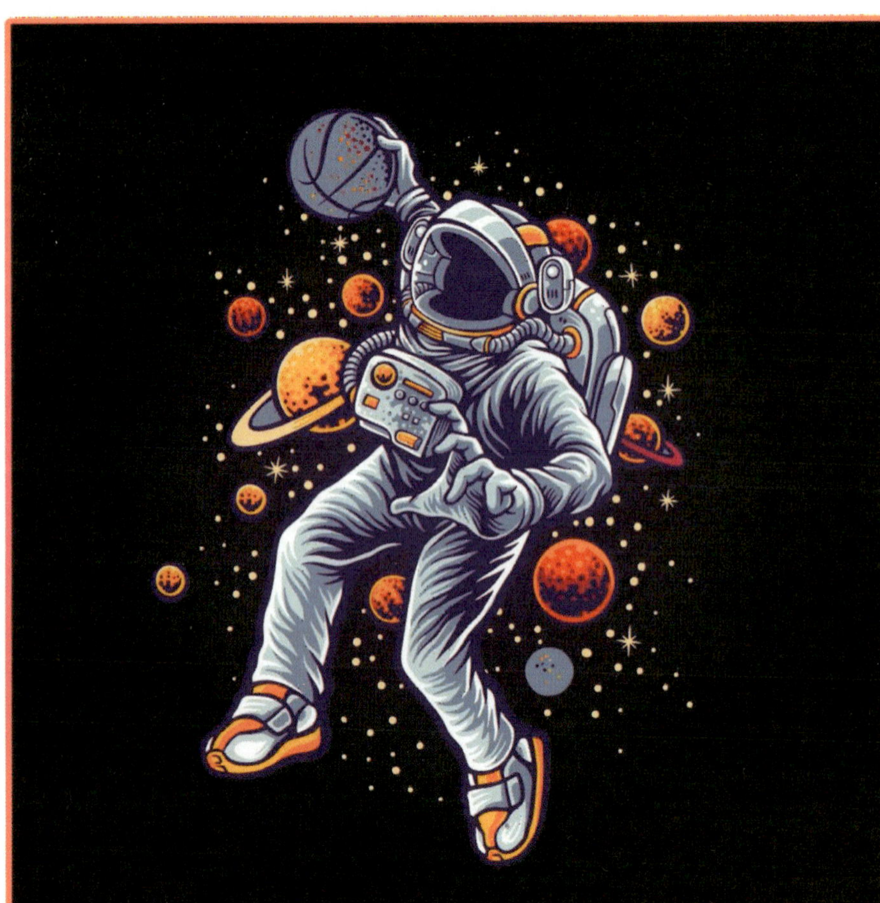

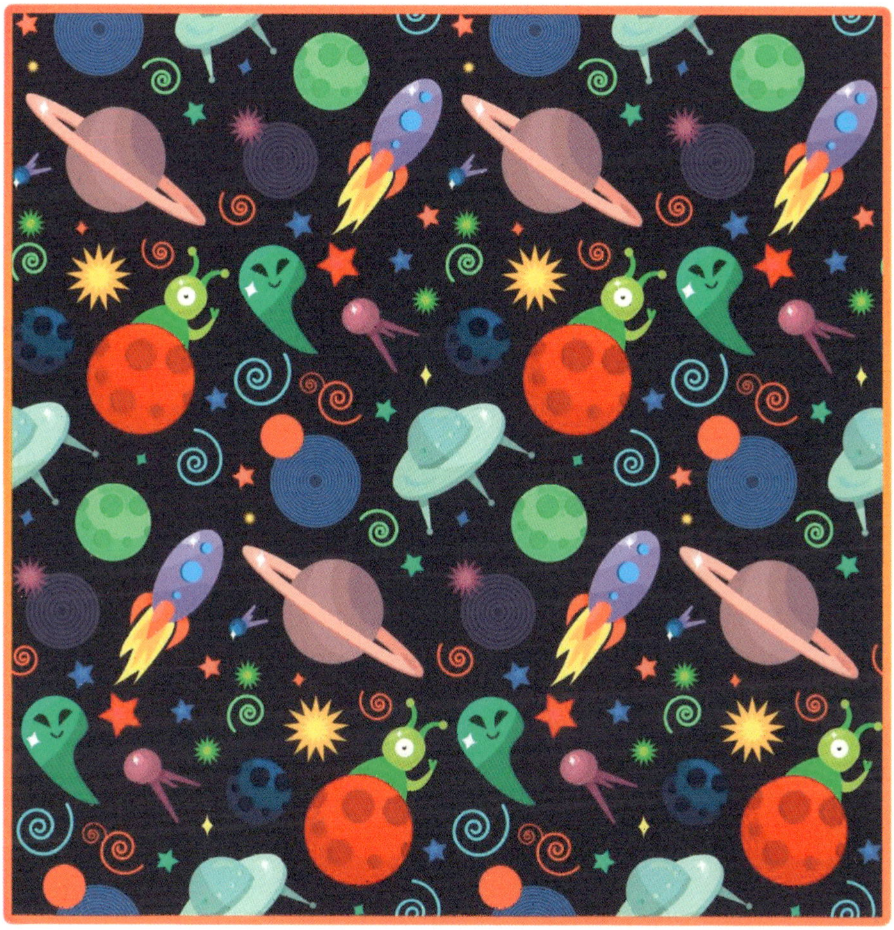

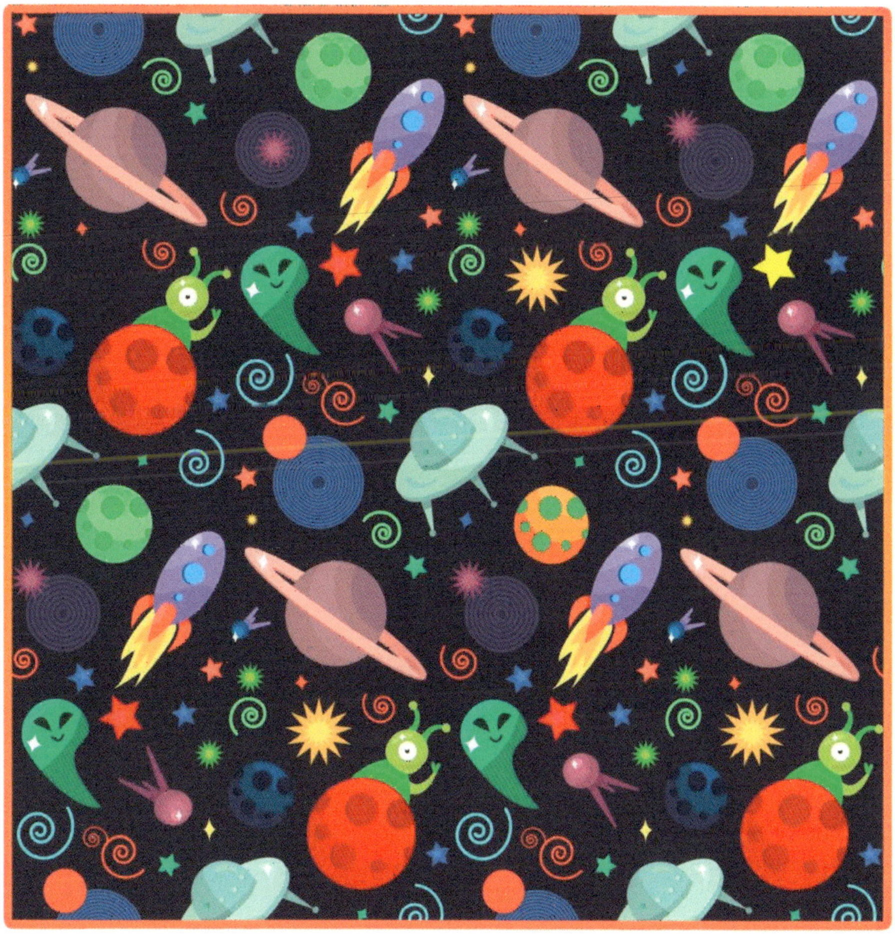

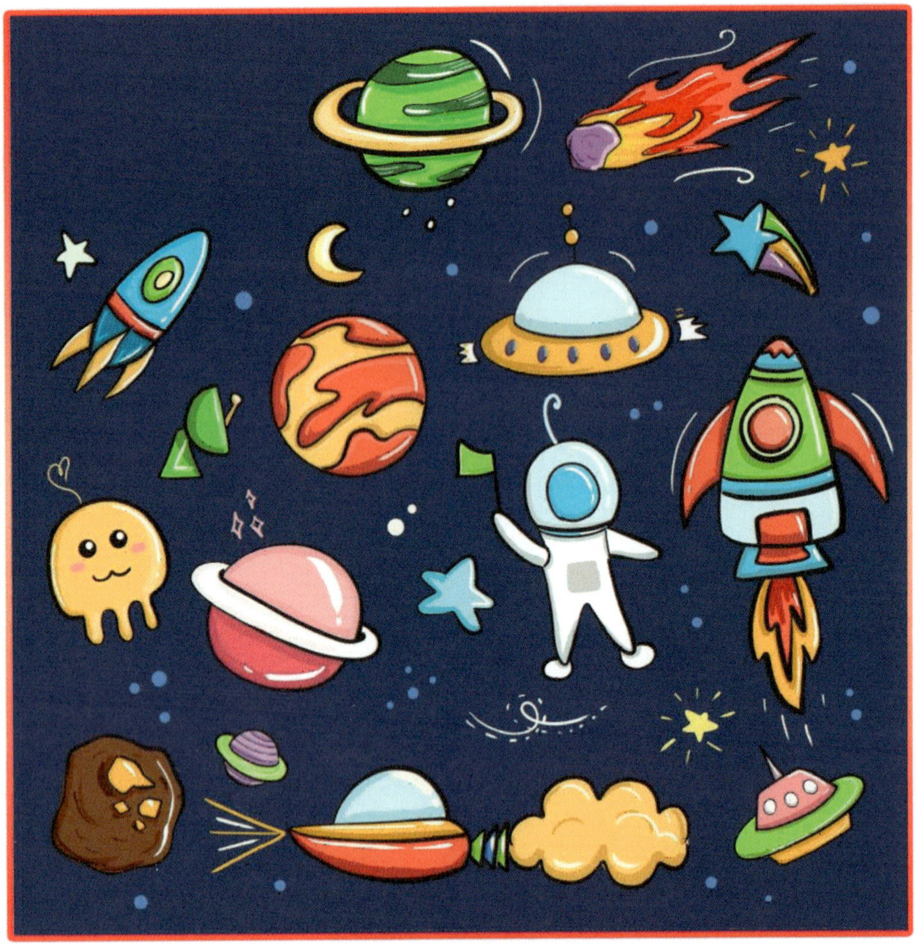

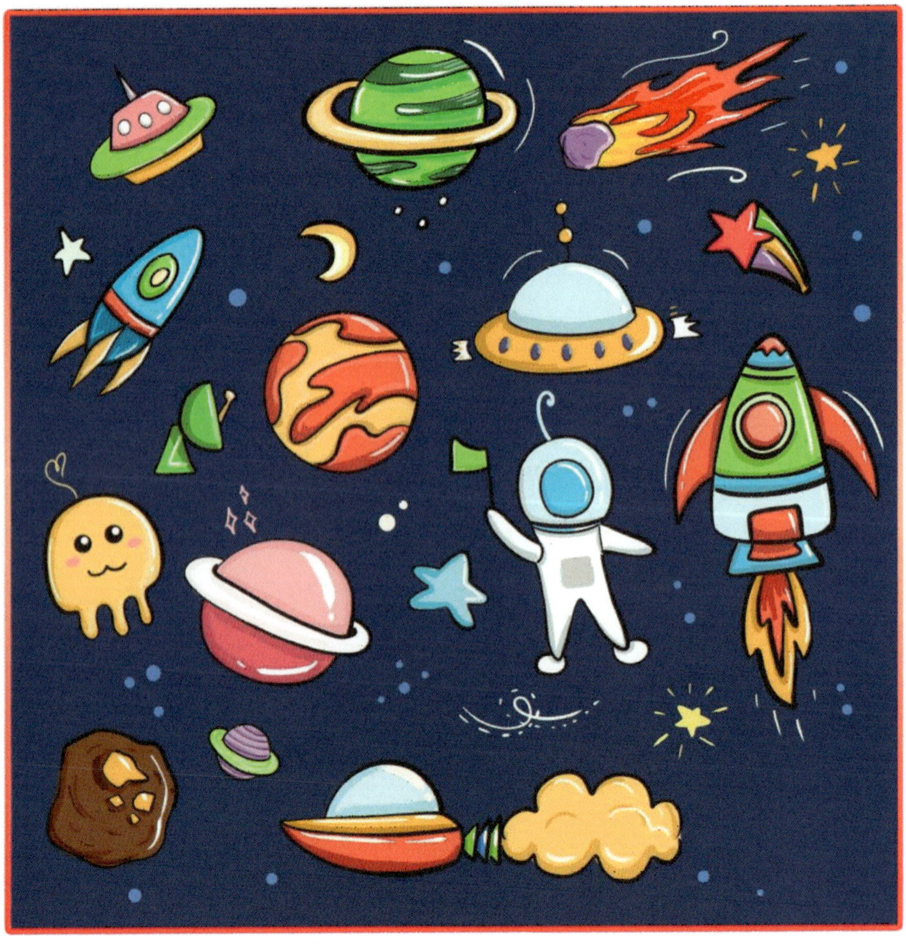

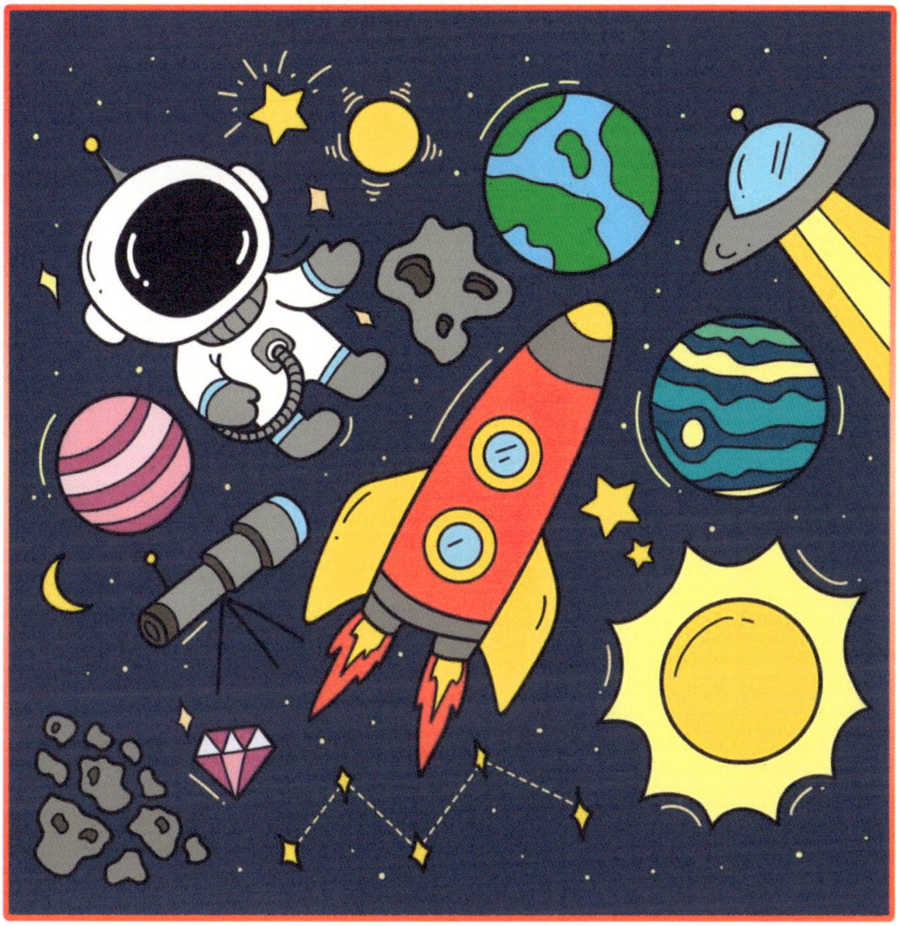

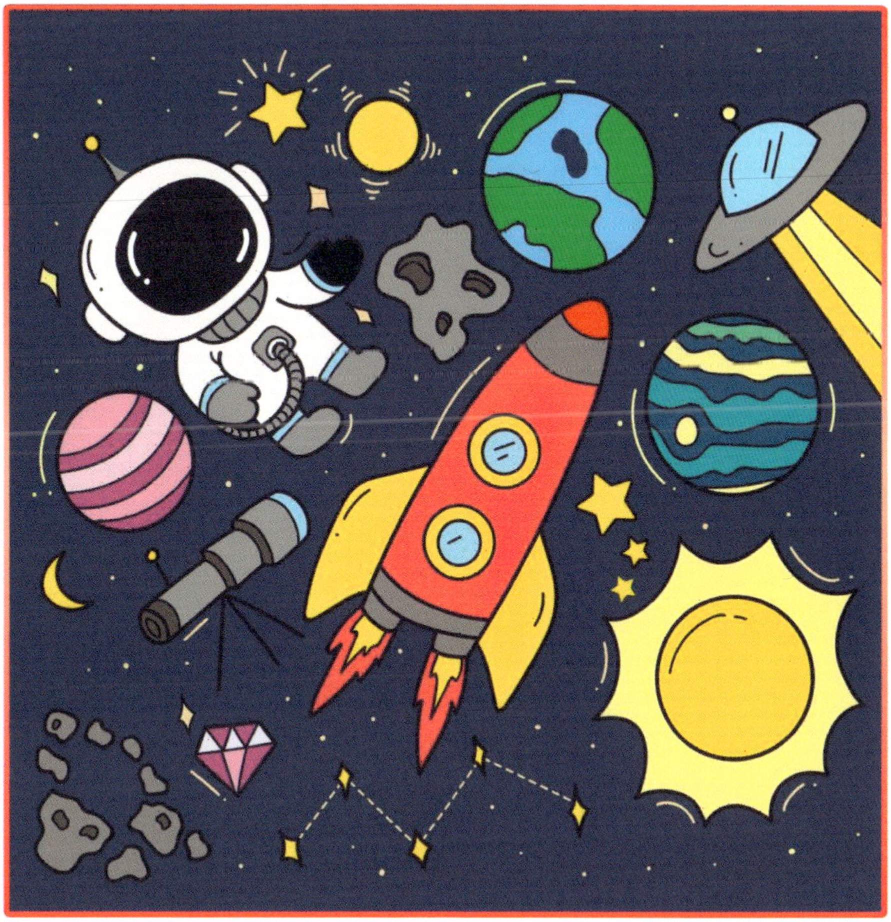

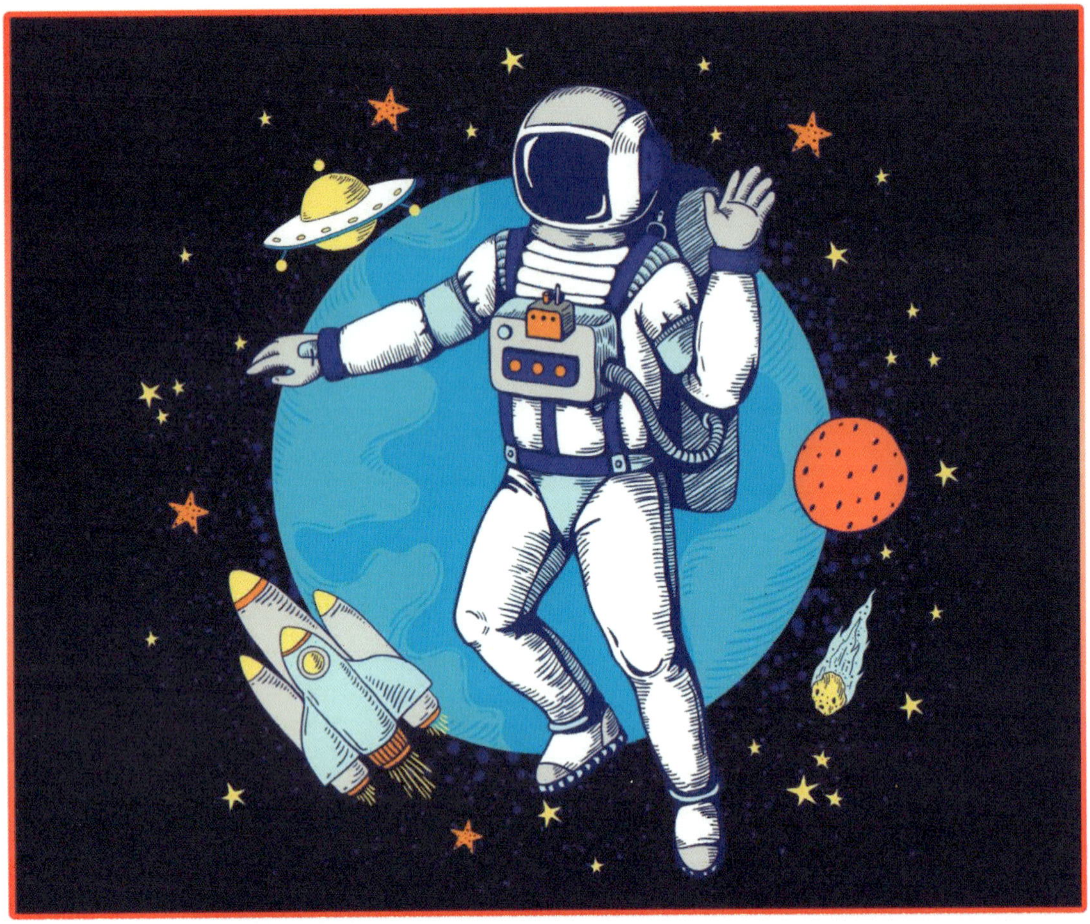

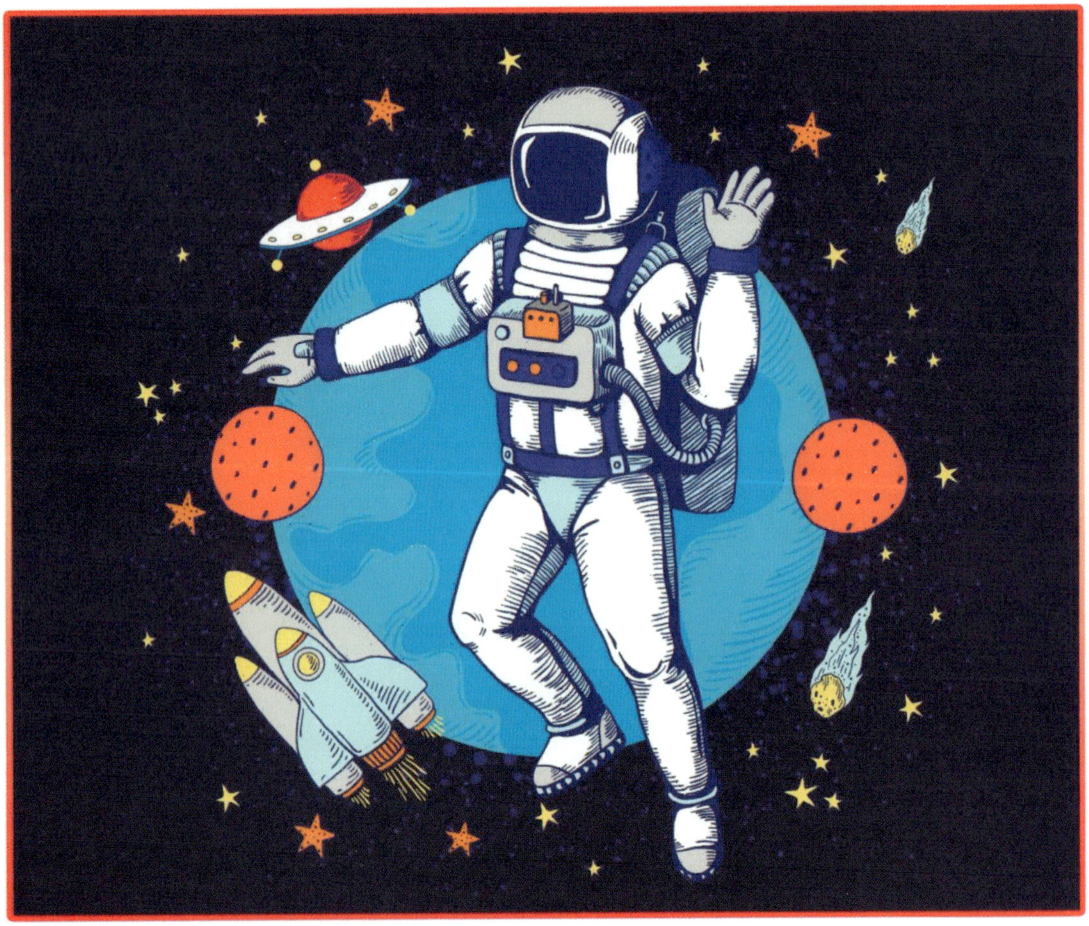

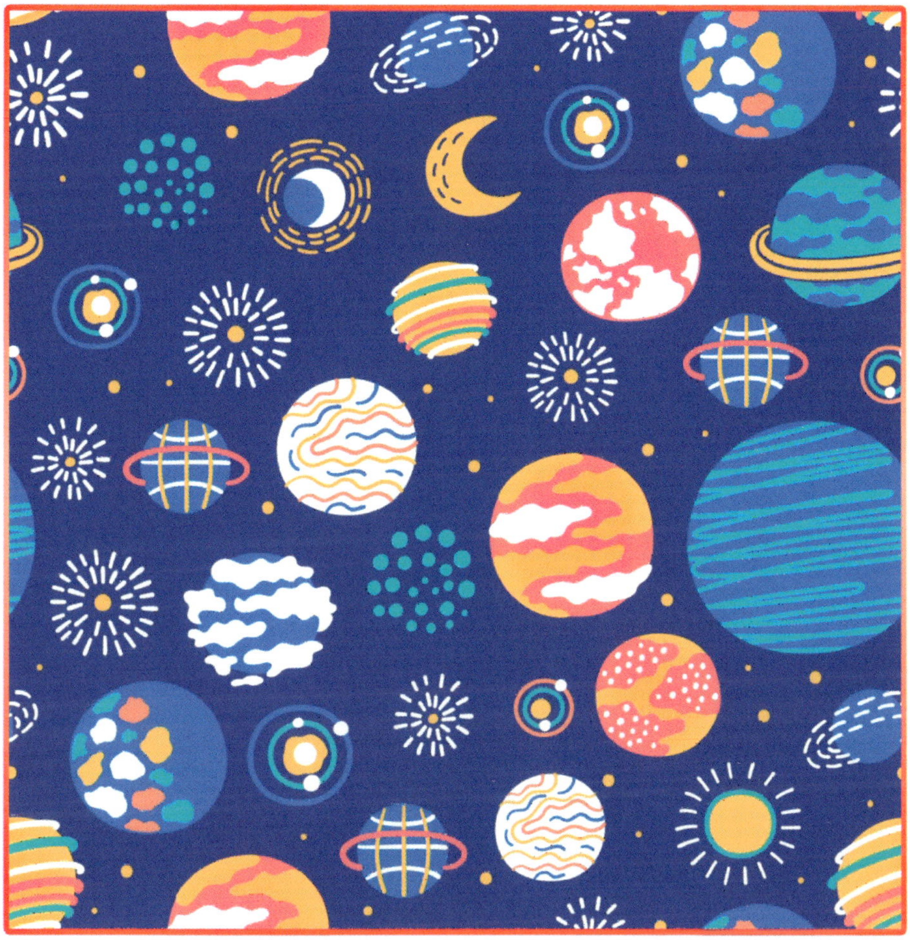

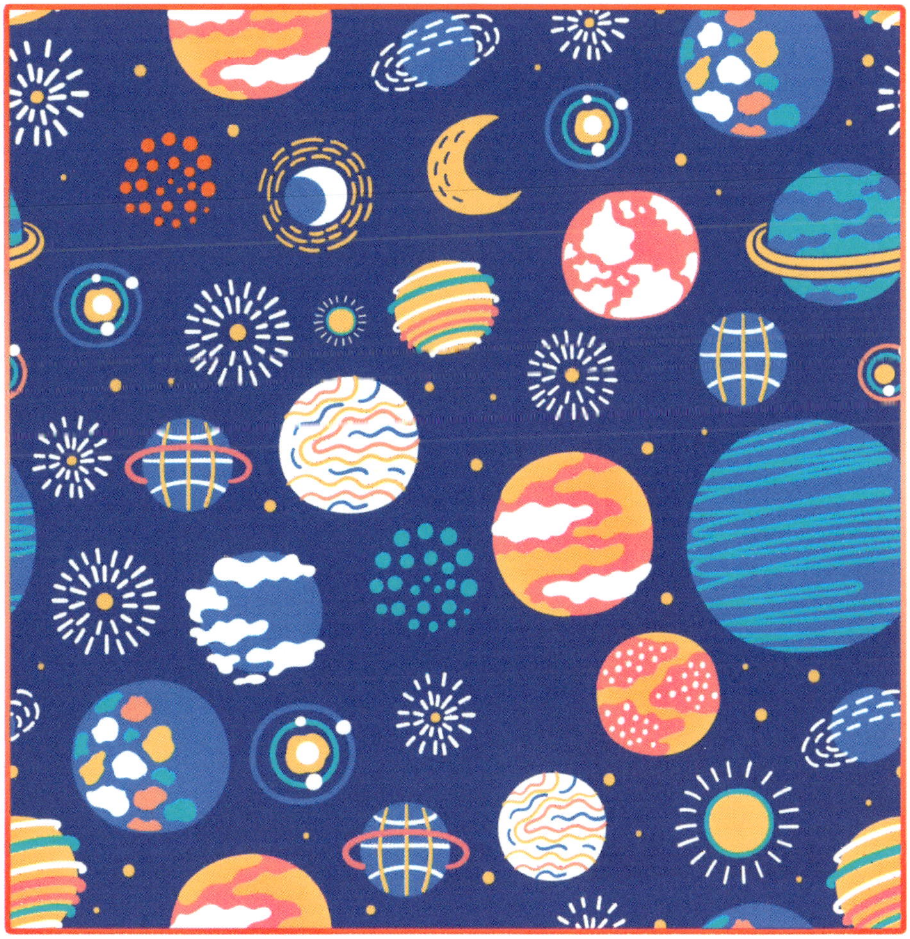

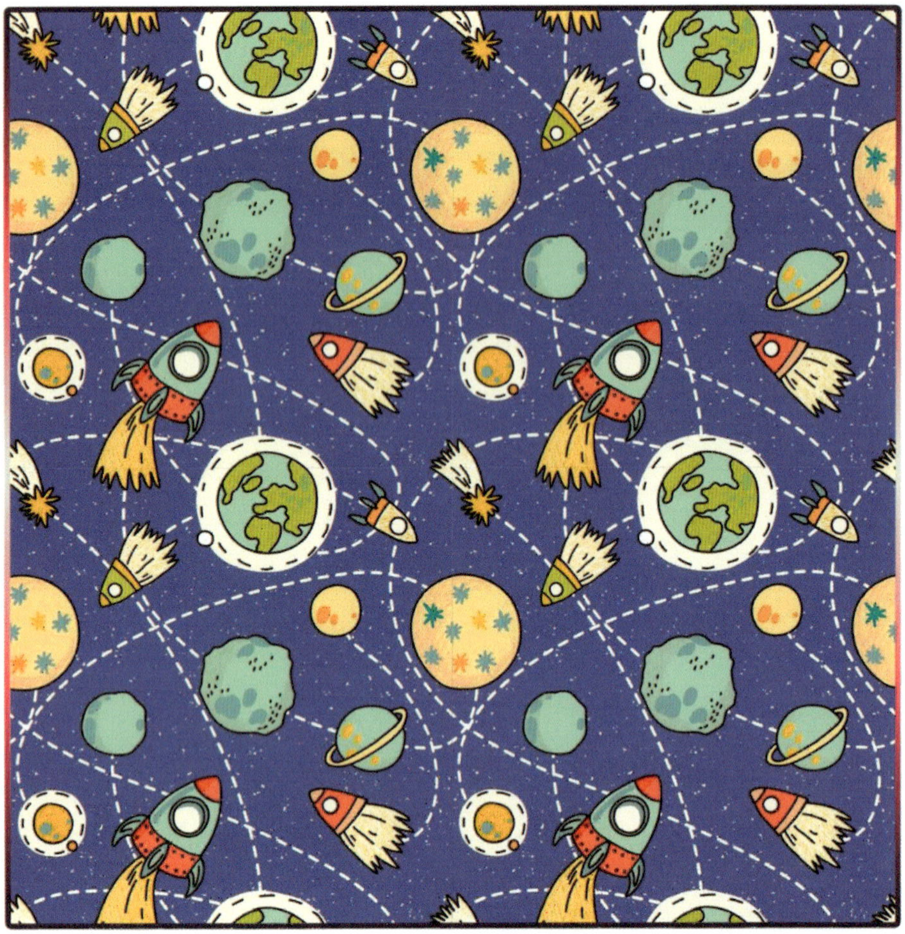

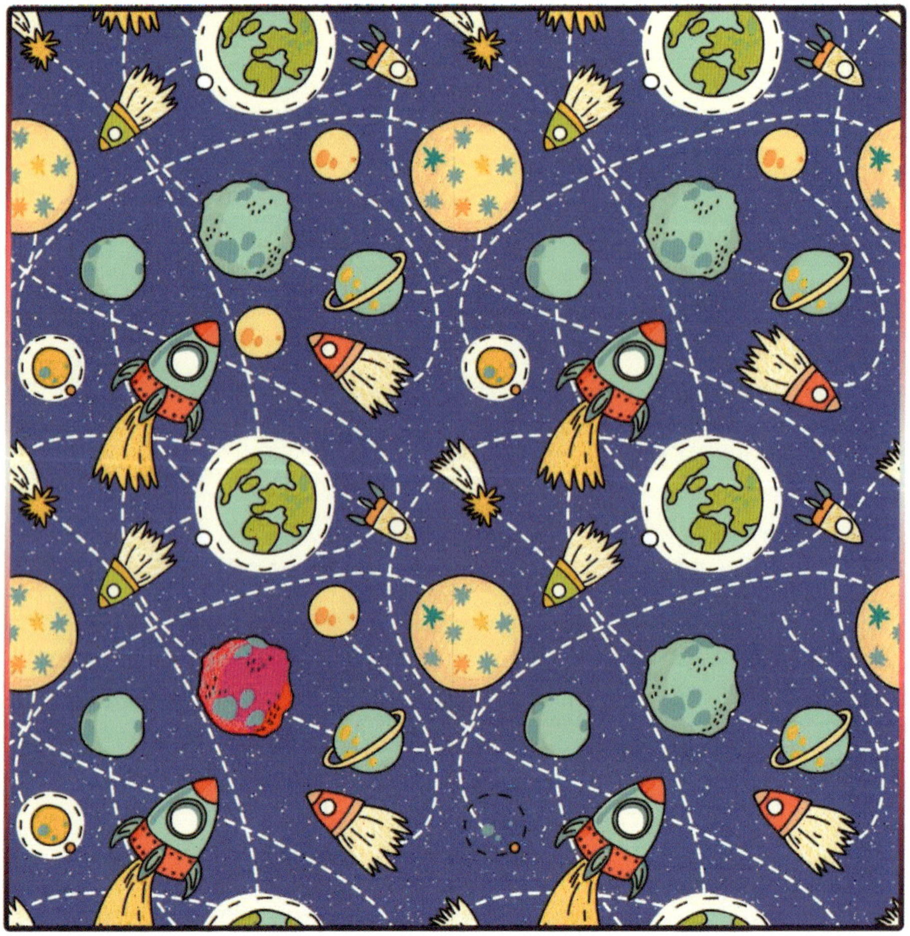

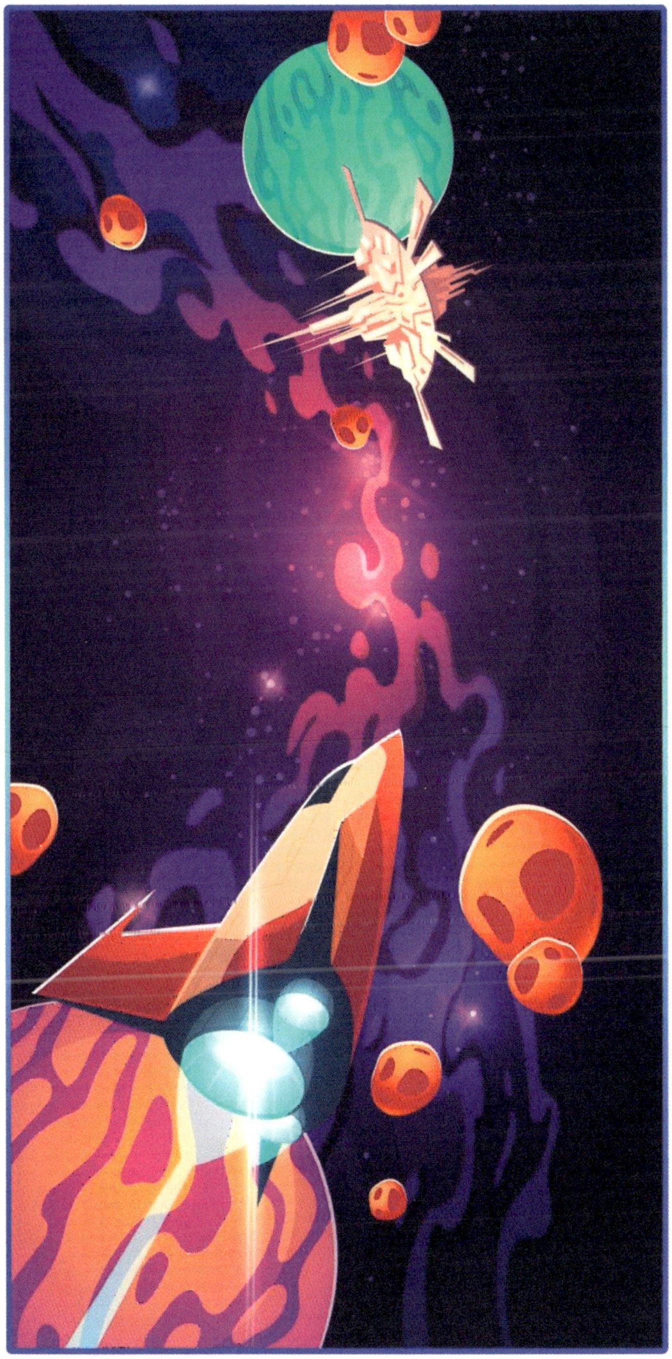

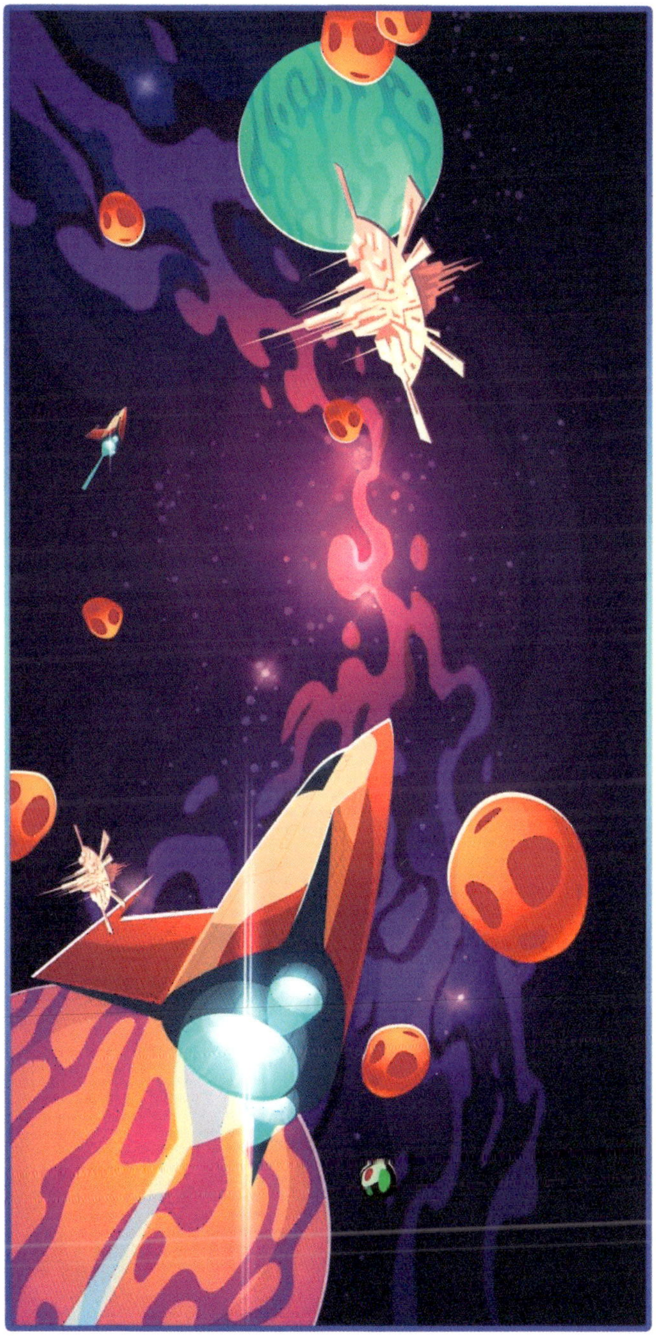

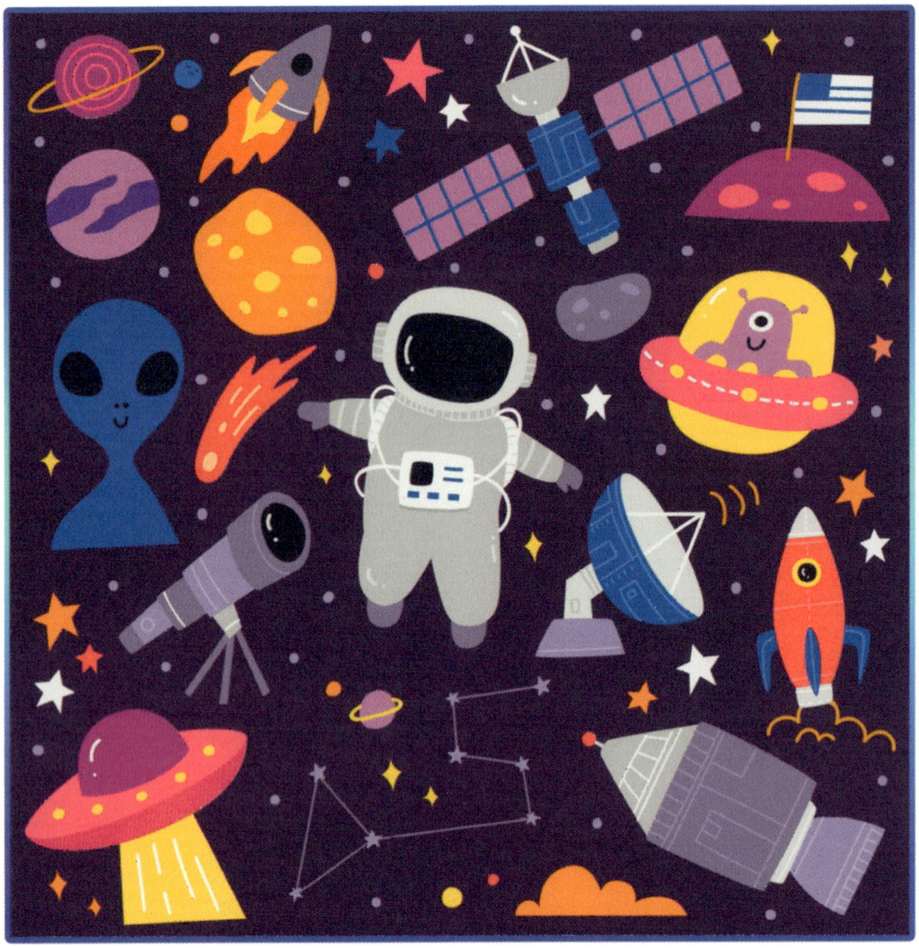

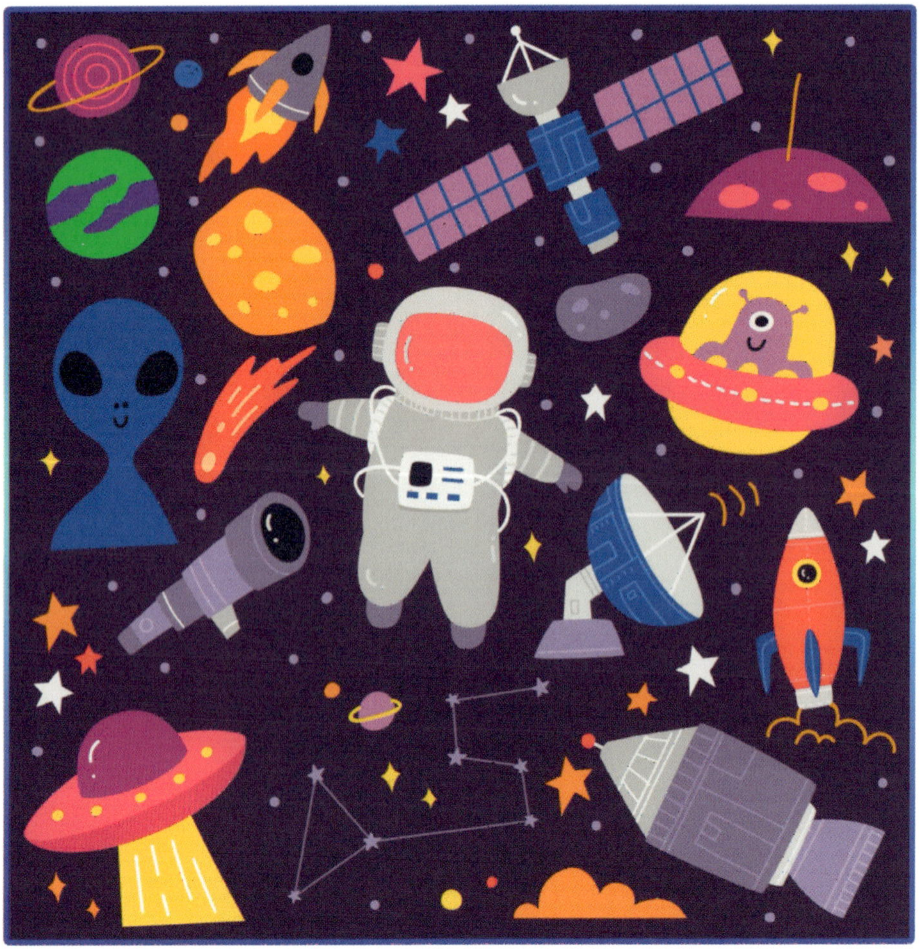

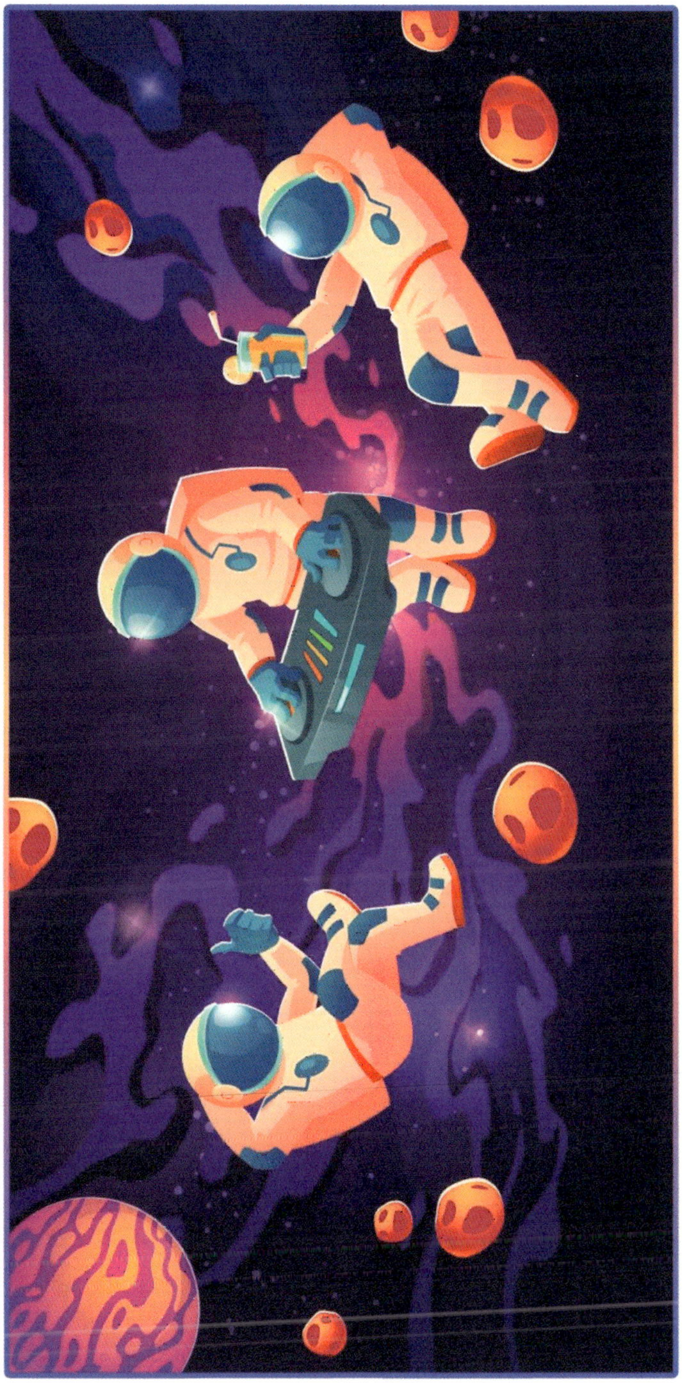

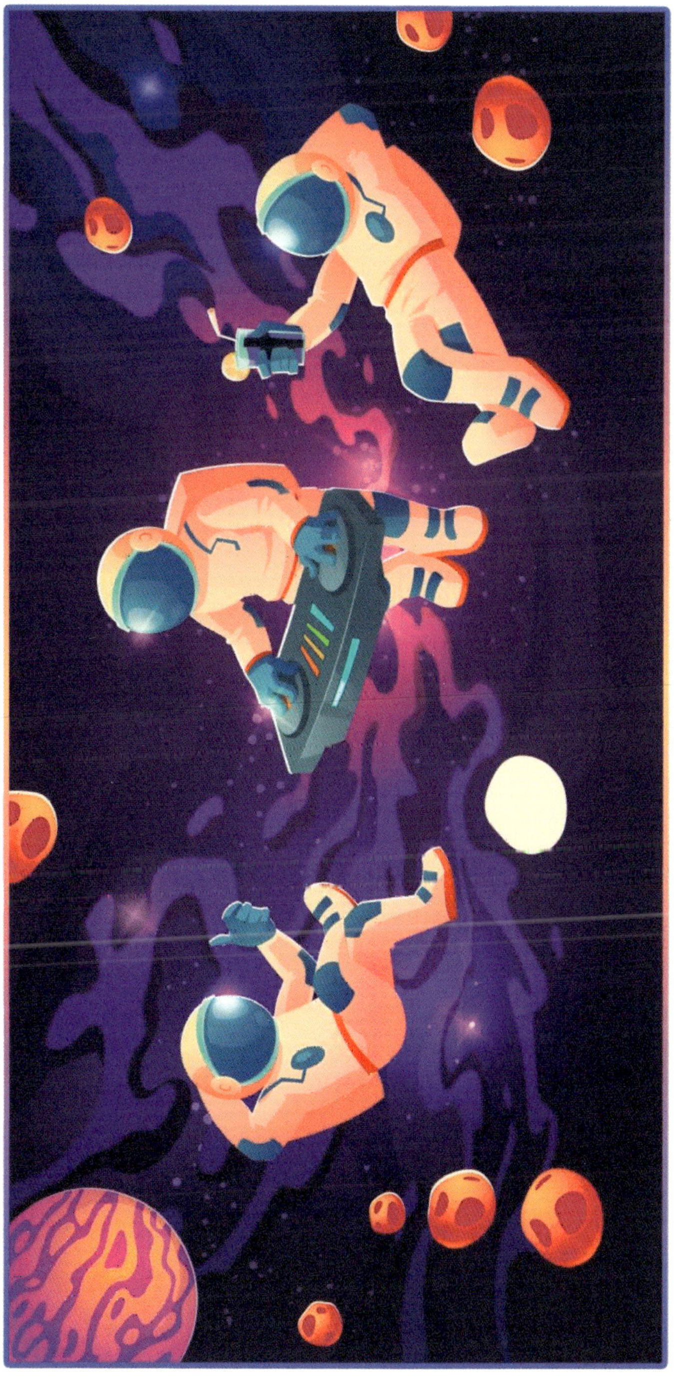

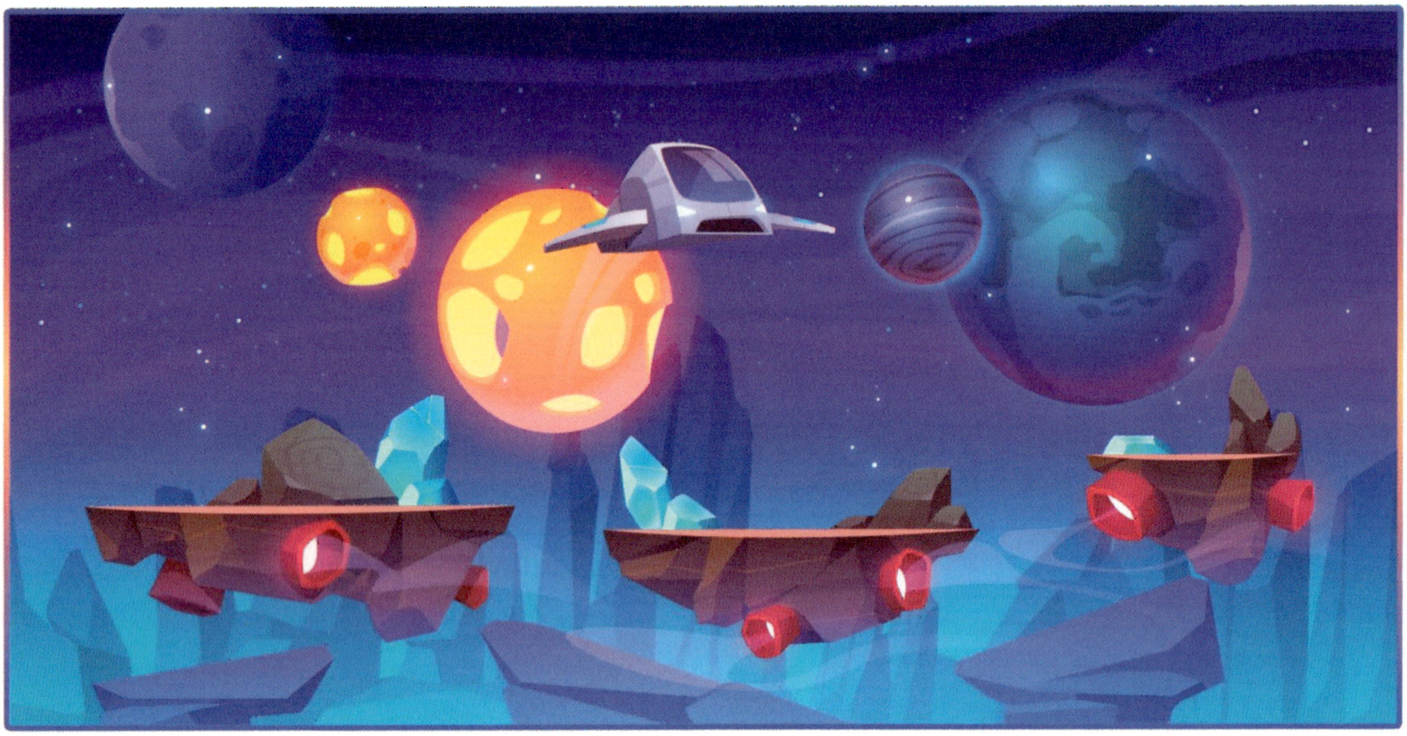

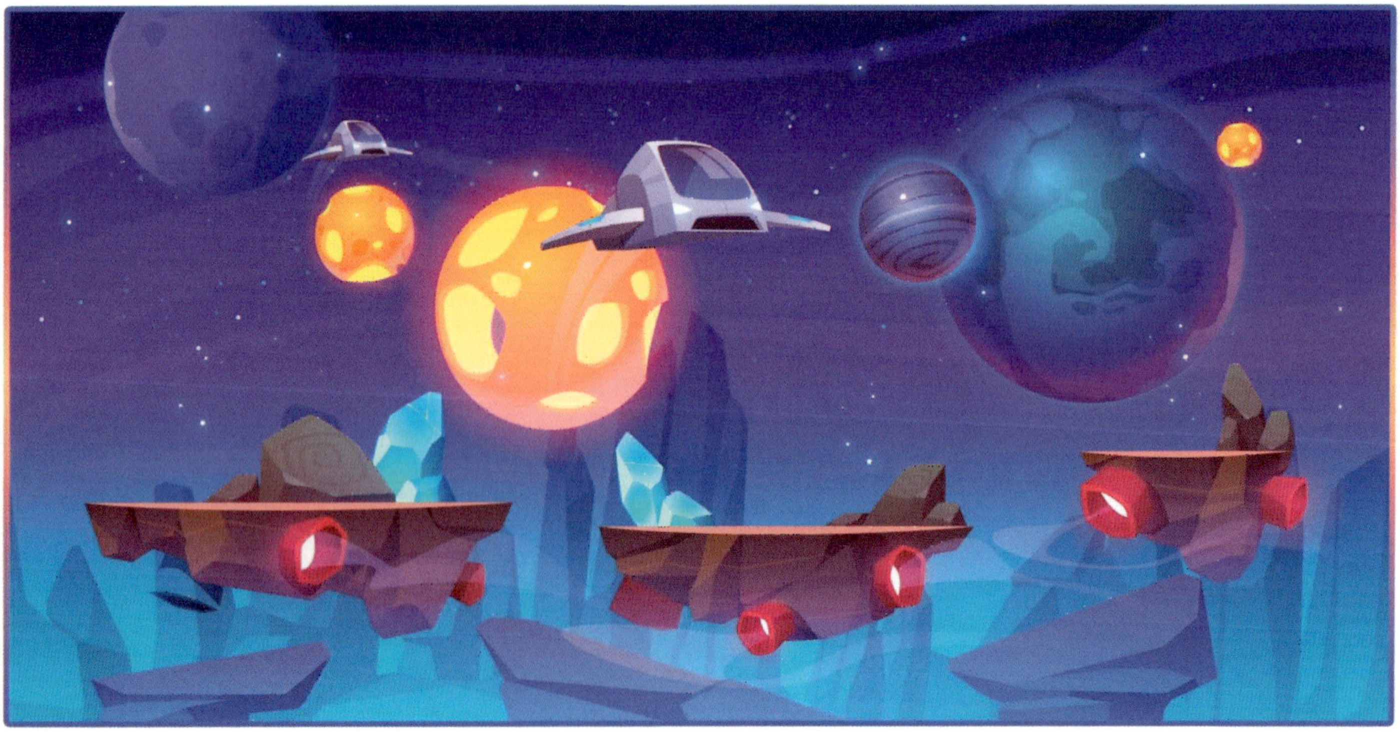

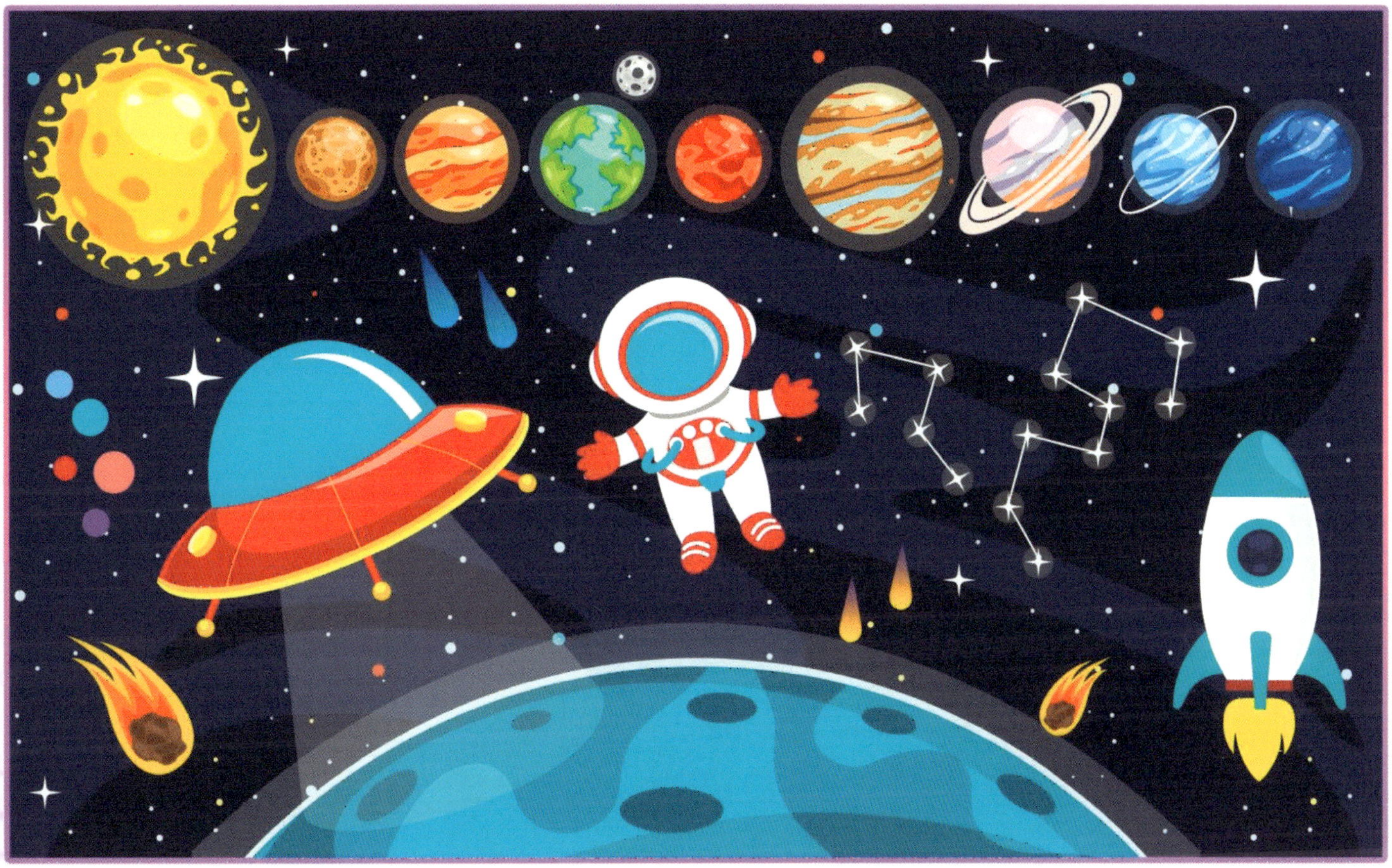

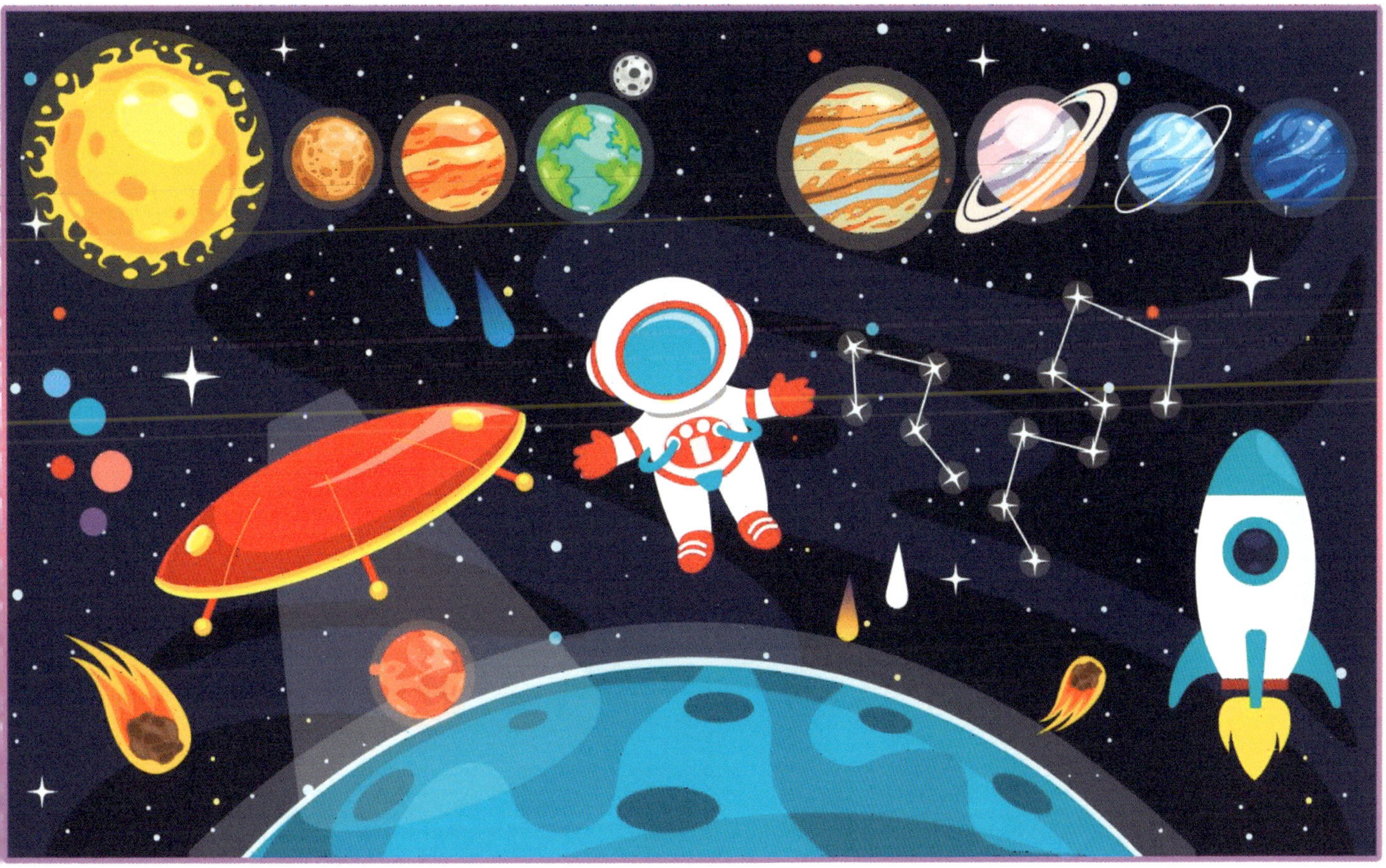

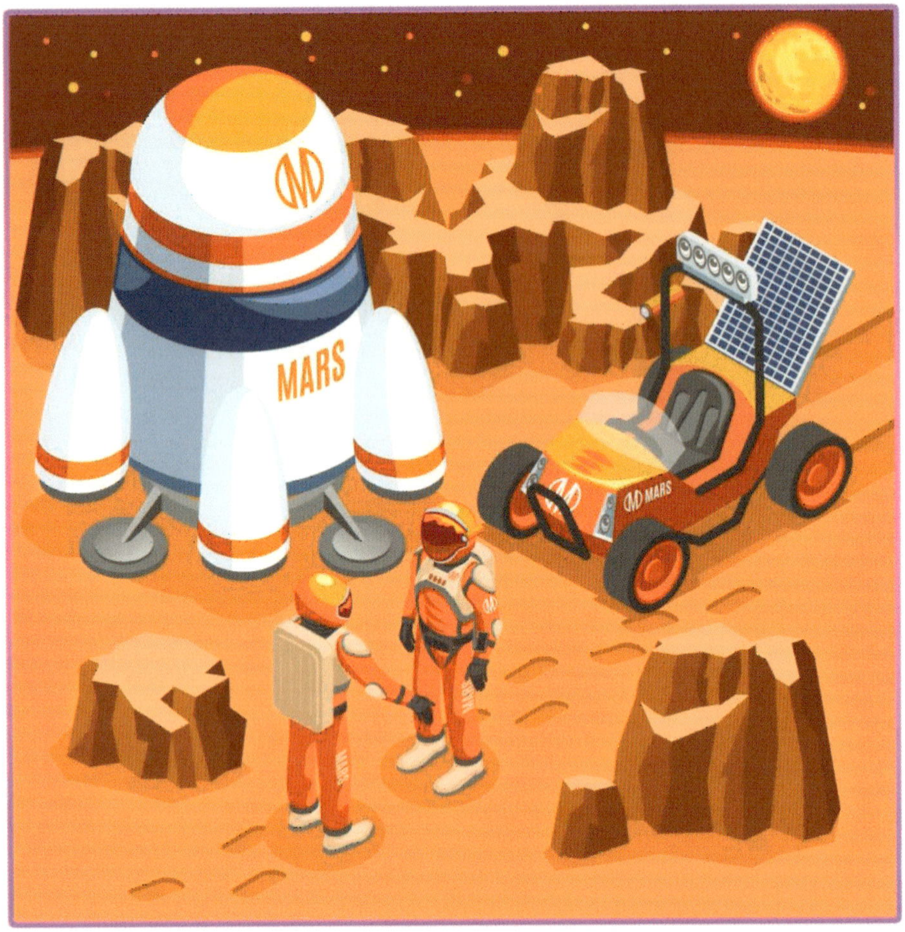
MARS
MARS

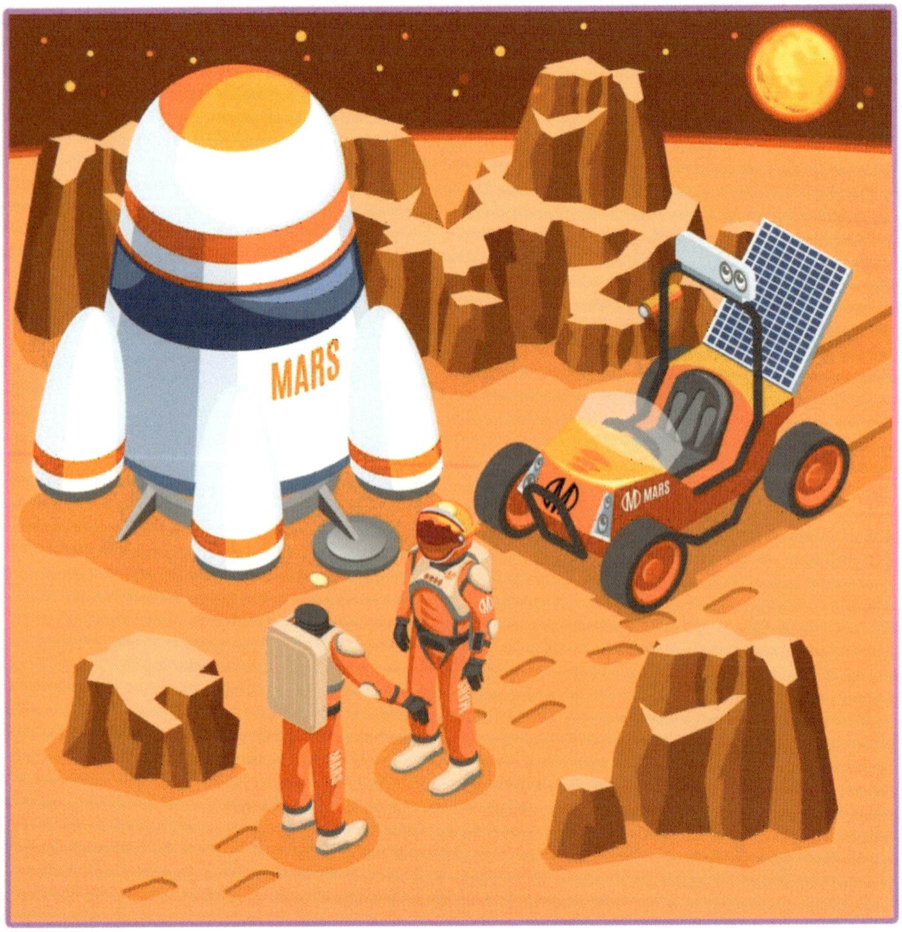
MARS
MARS

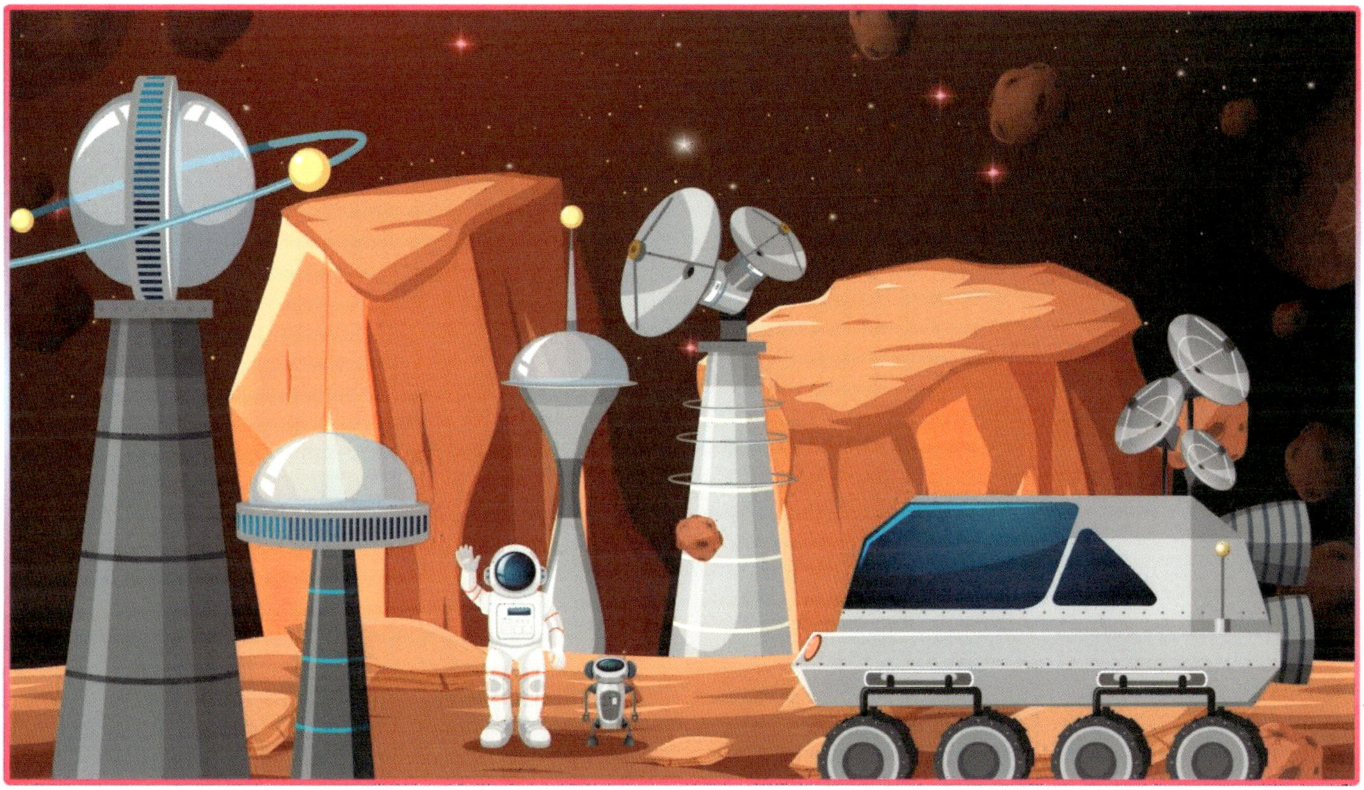

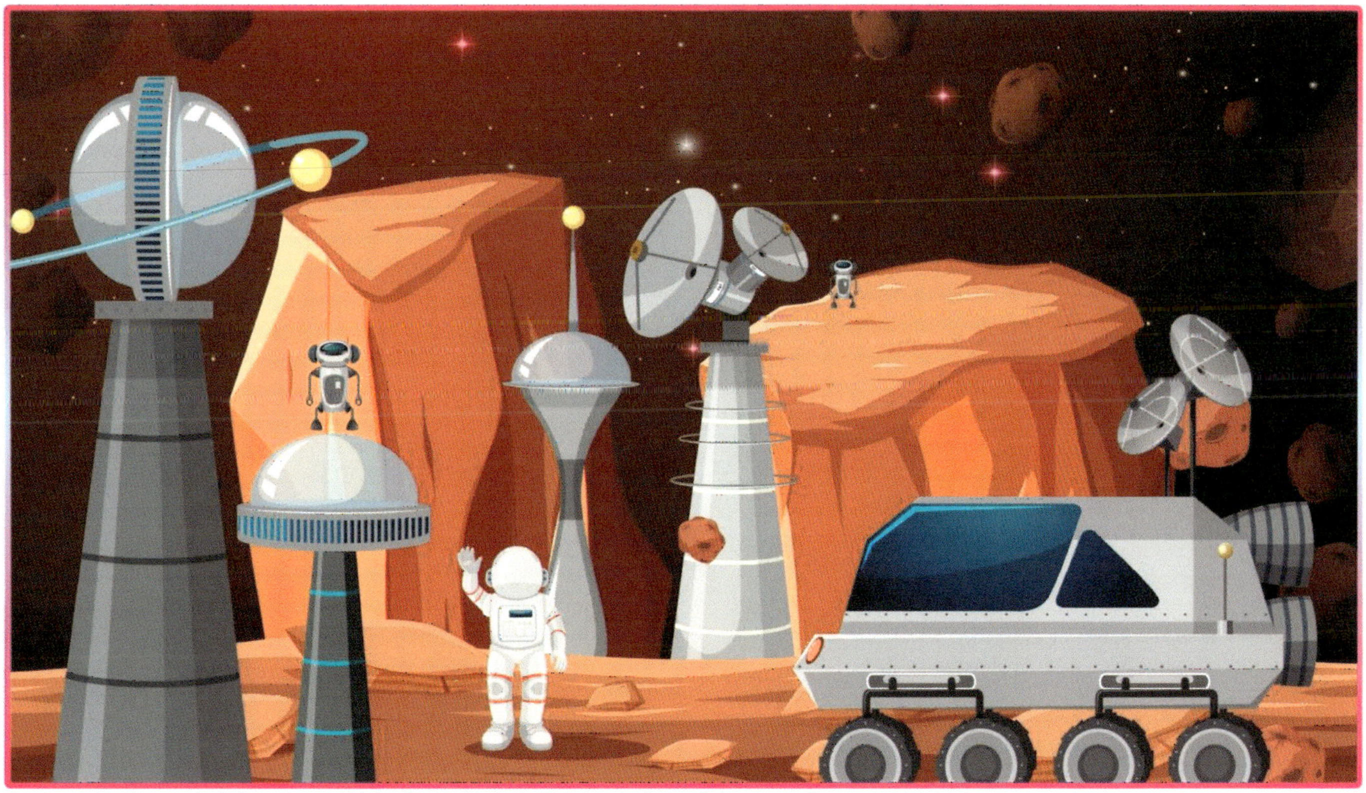

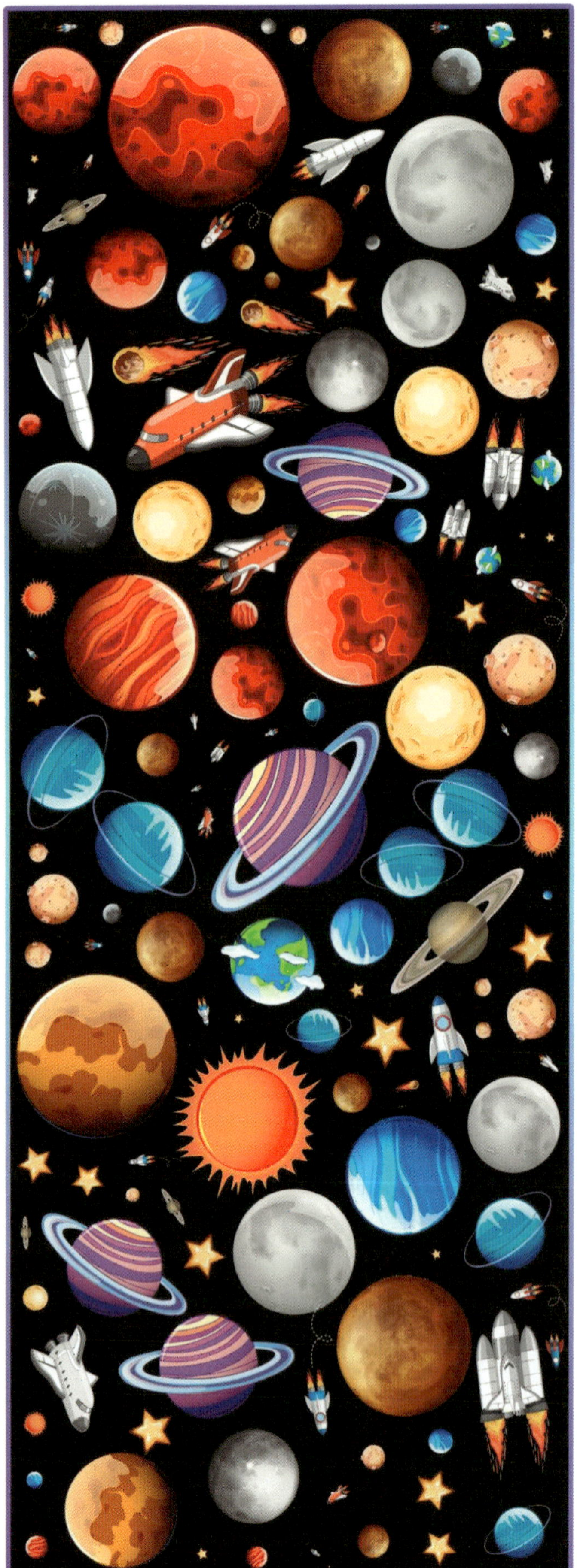

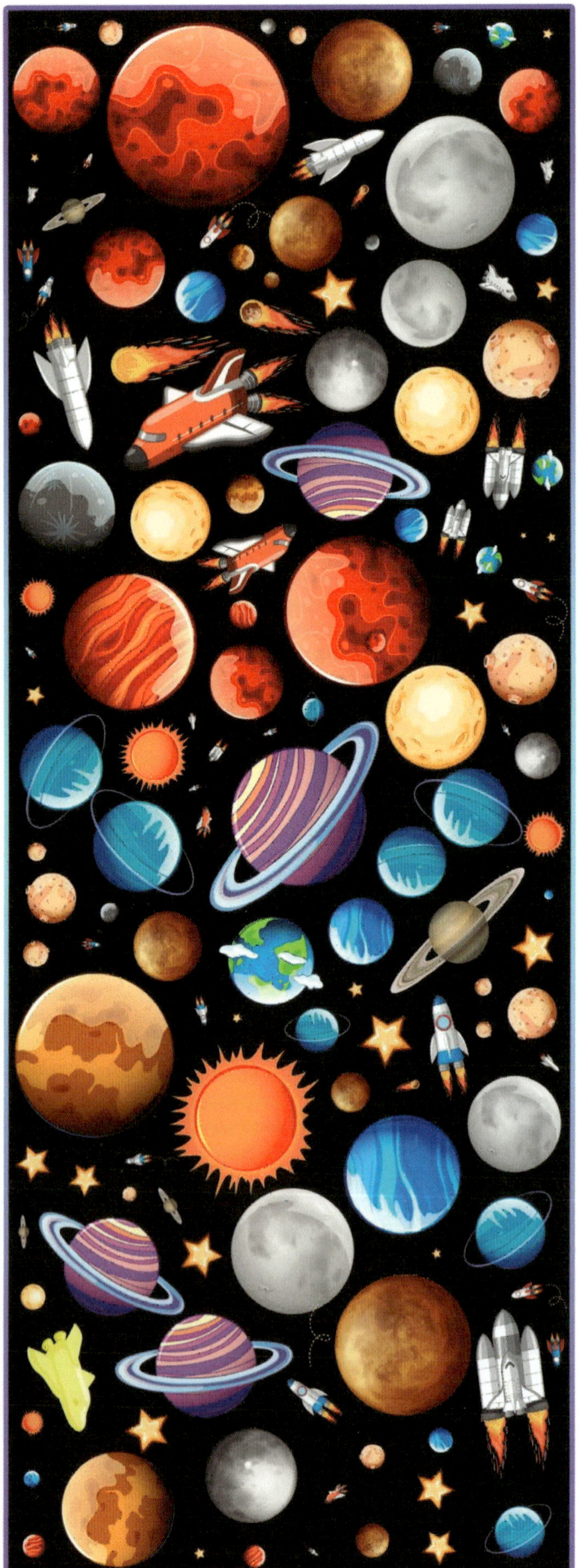

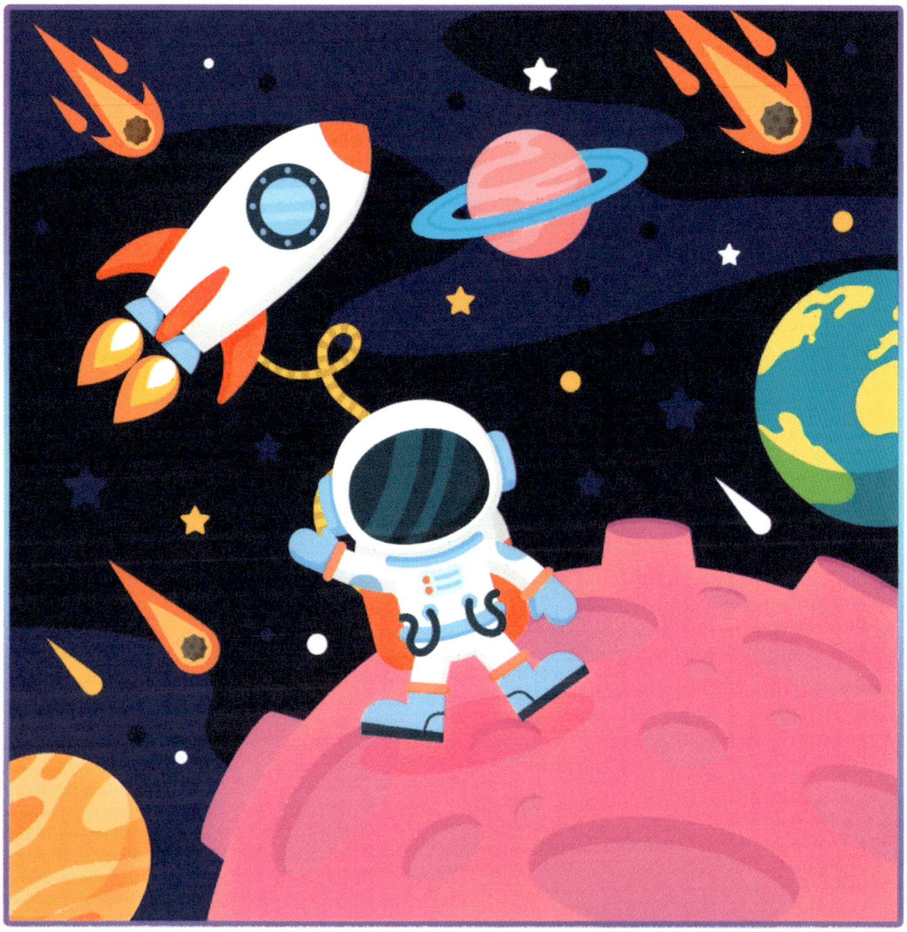
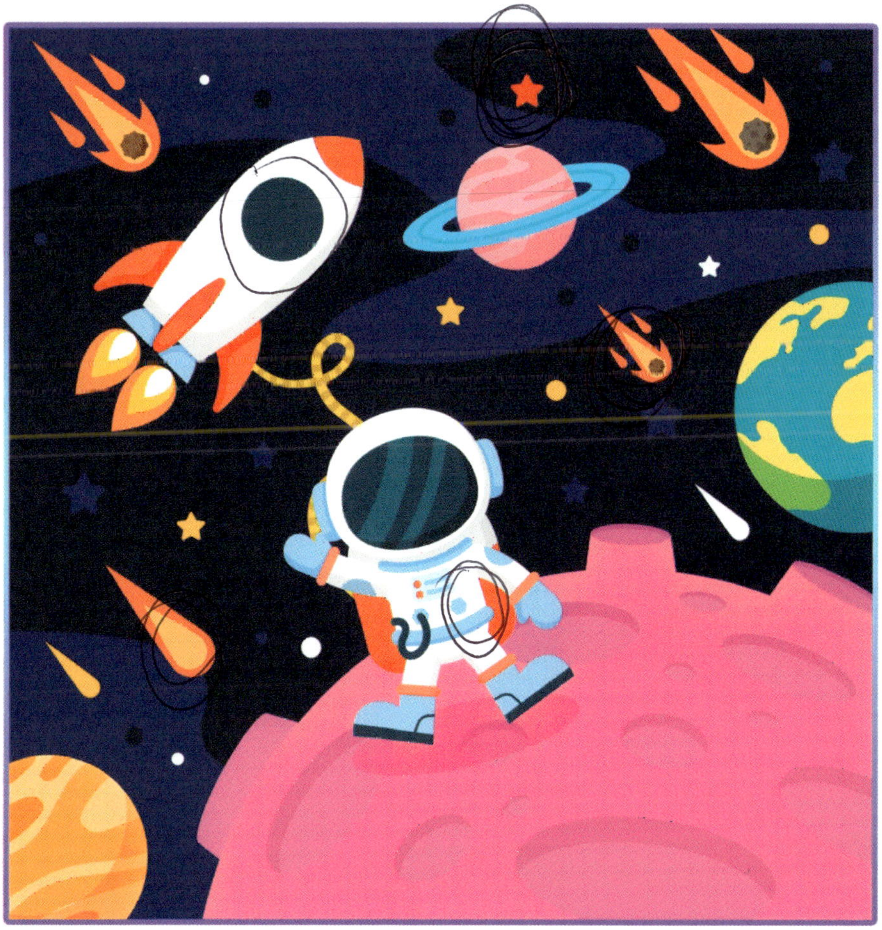

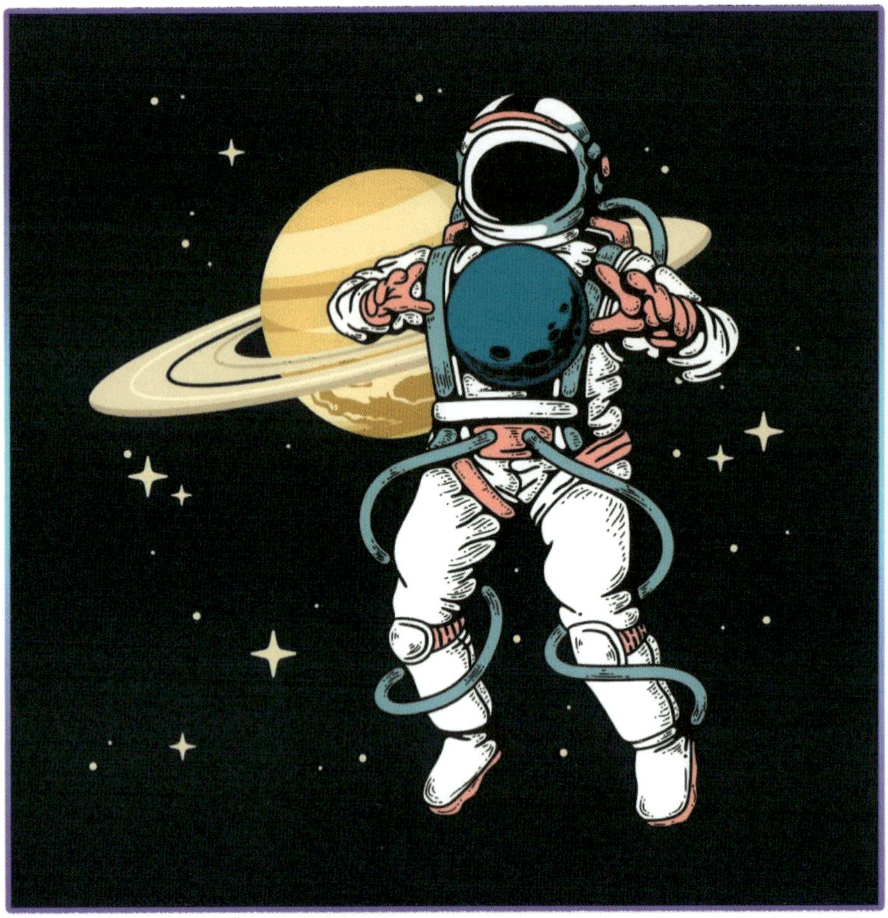

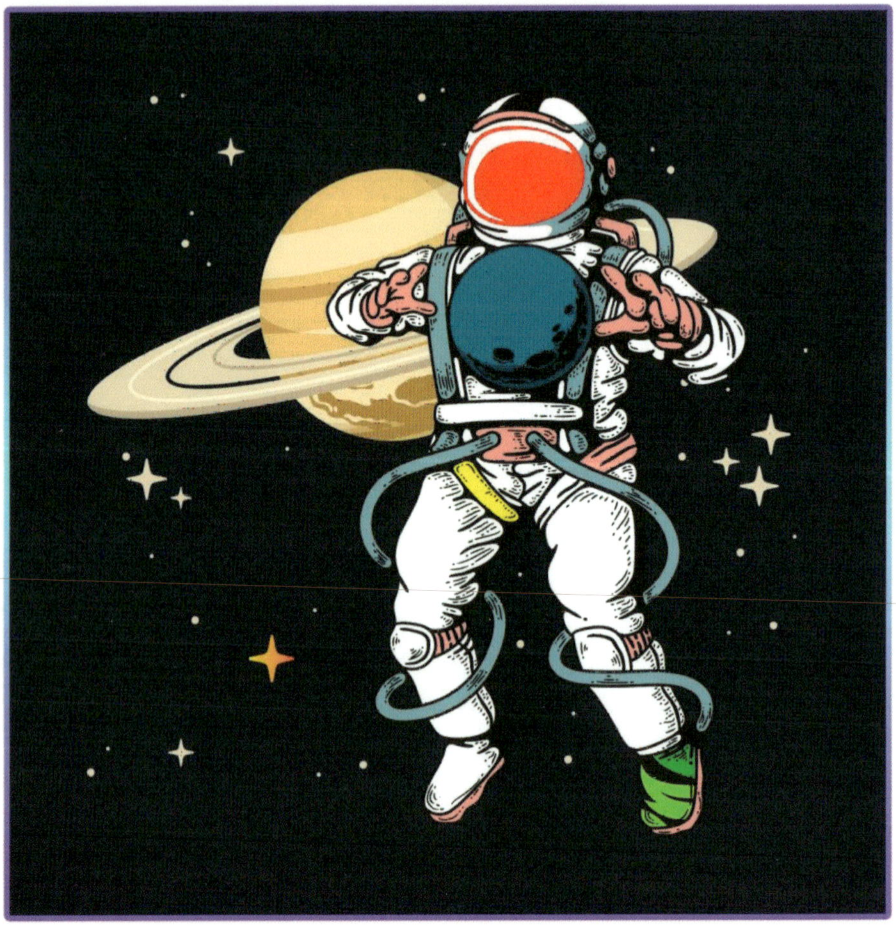

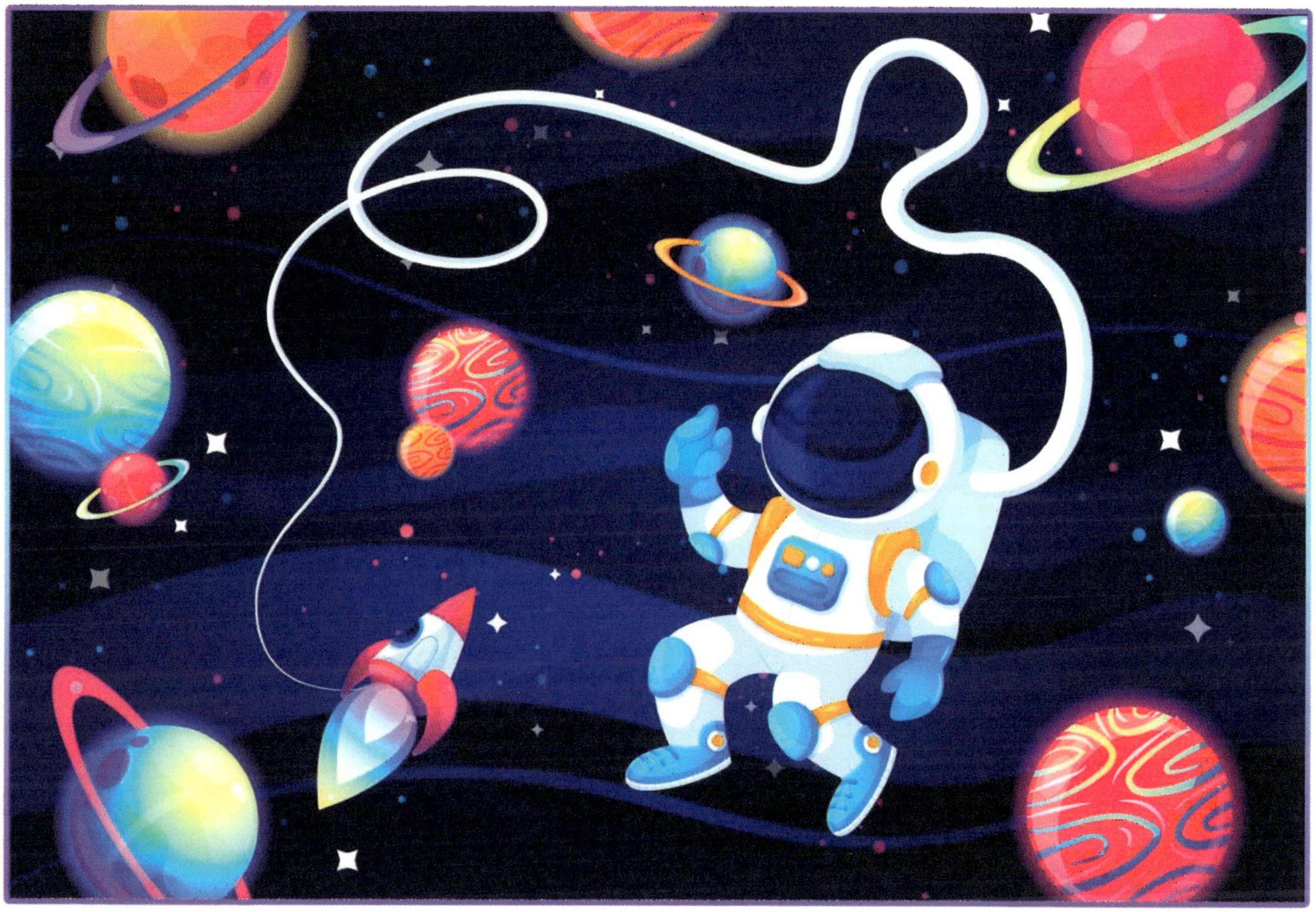

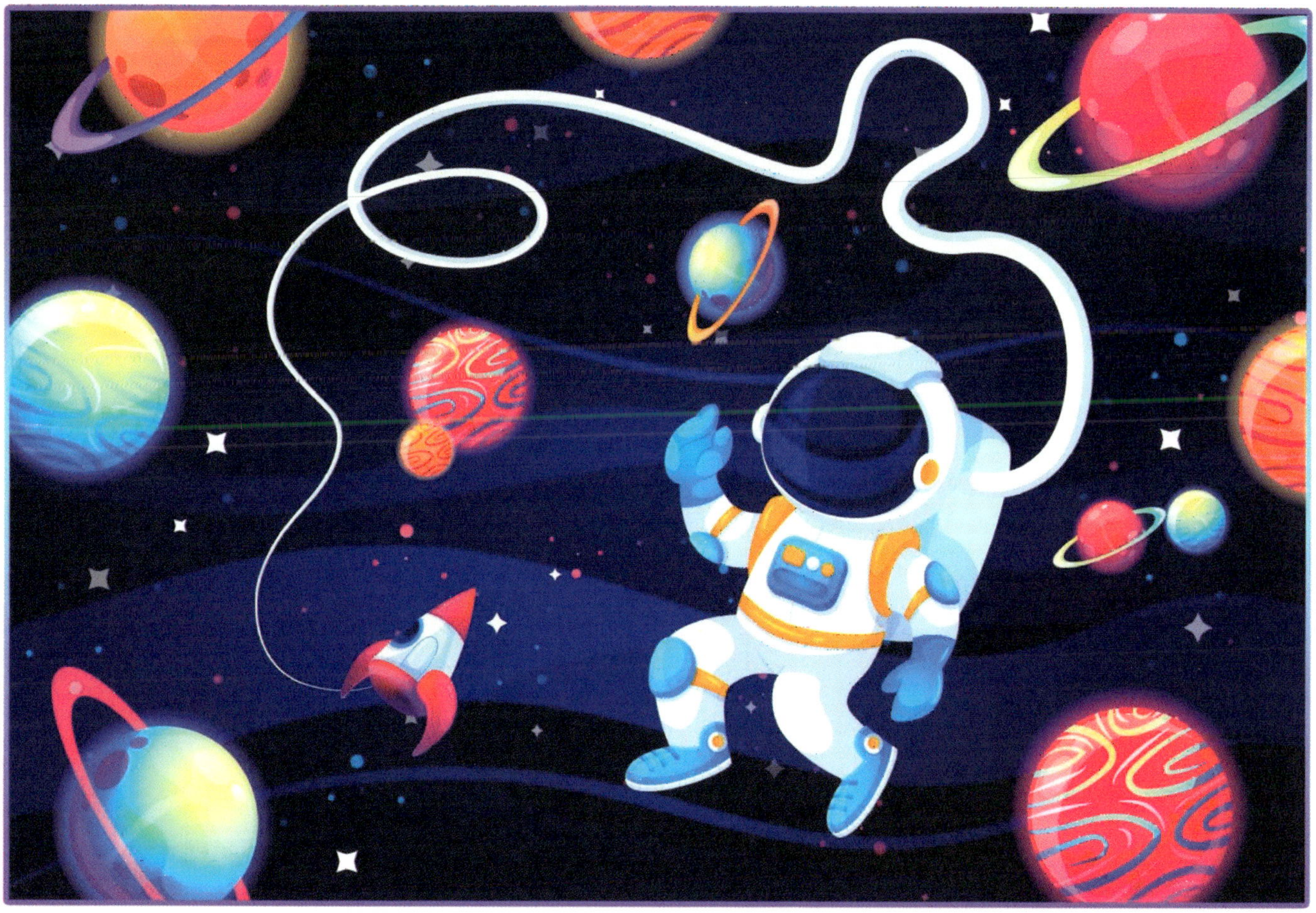

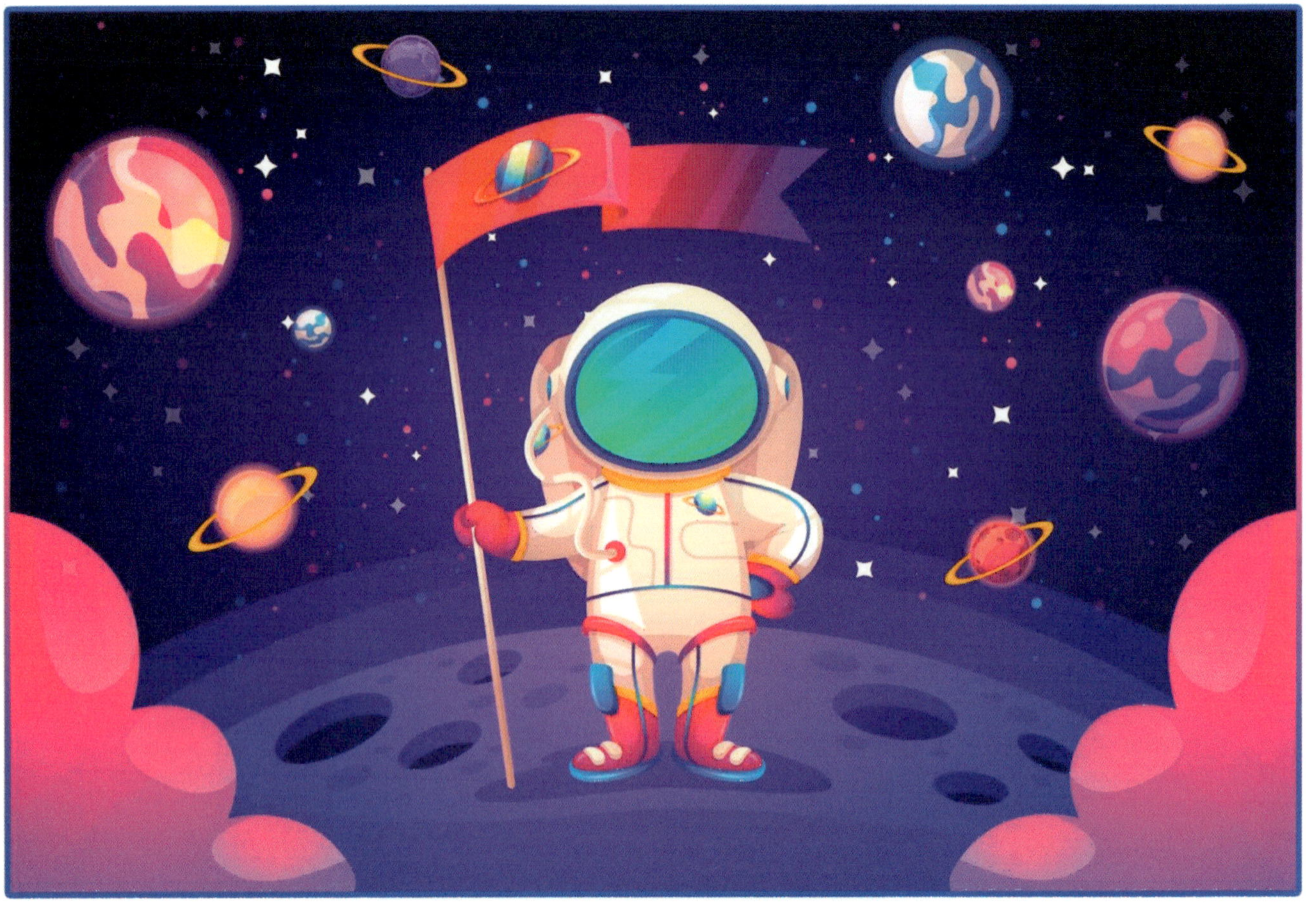

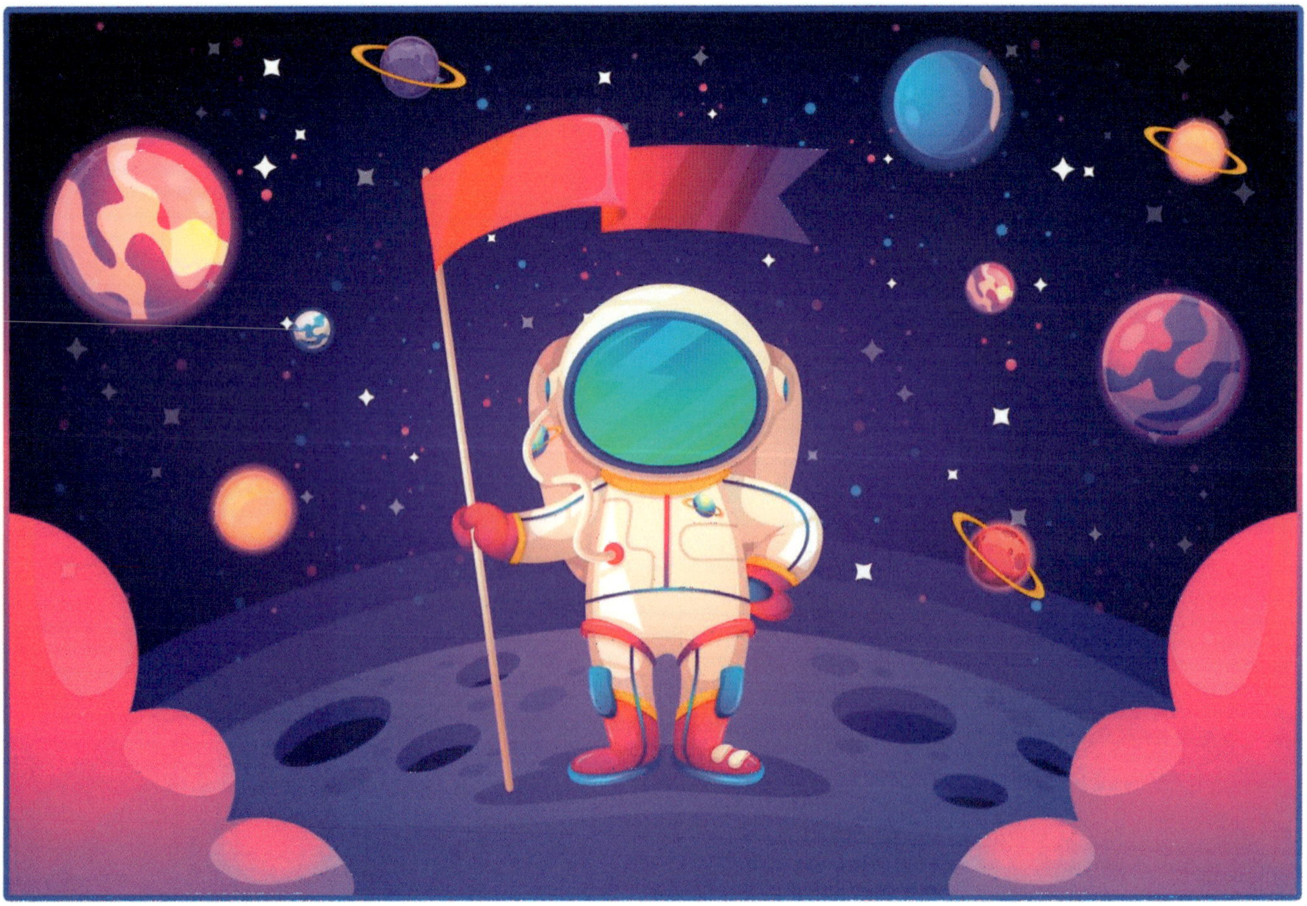

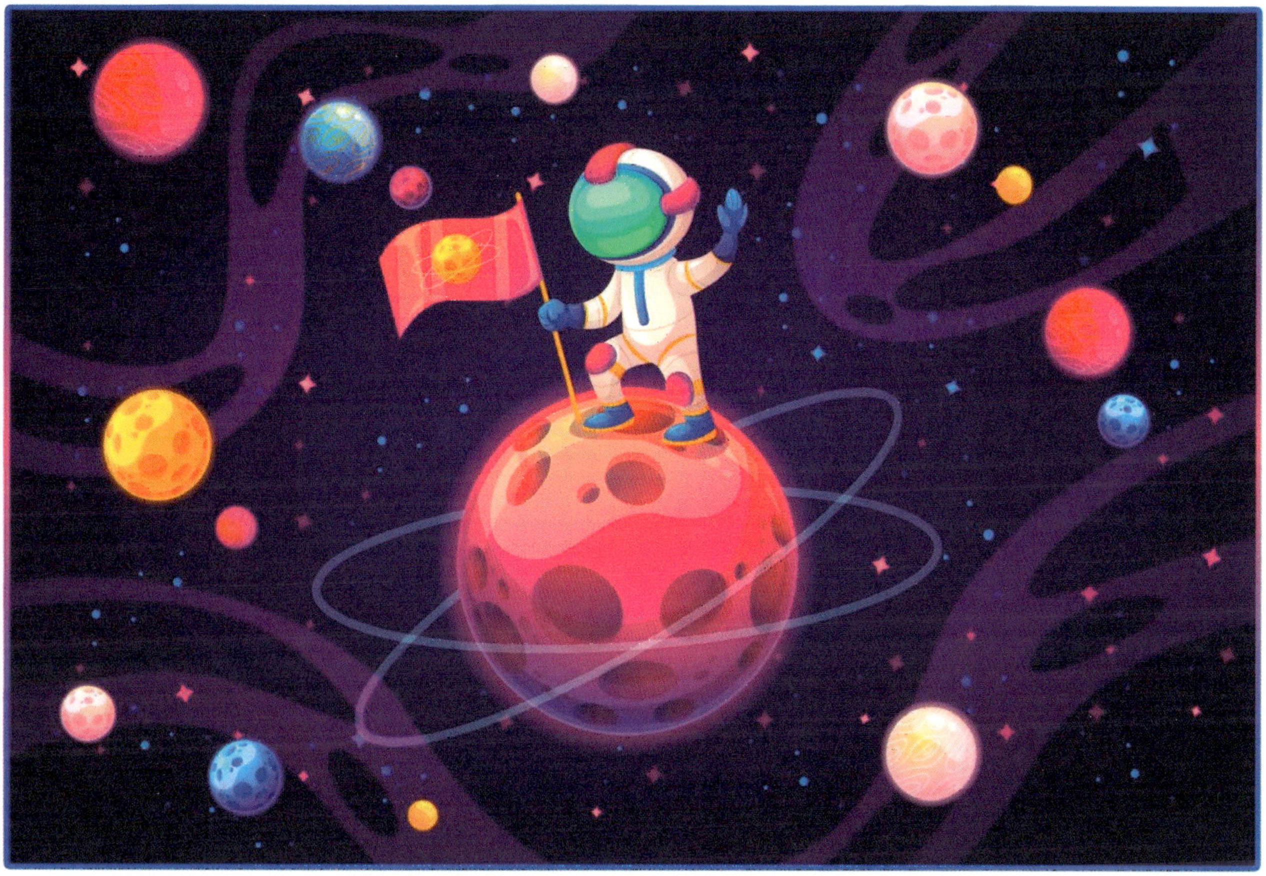

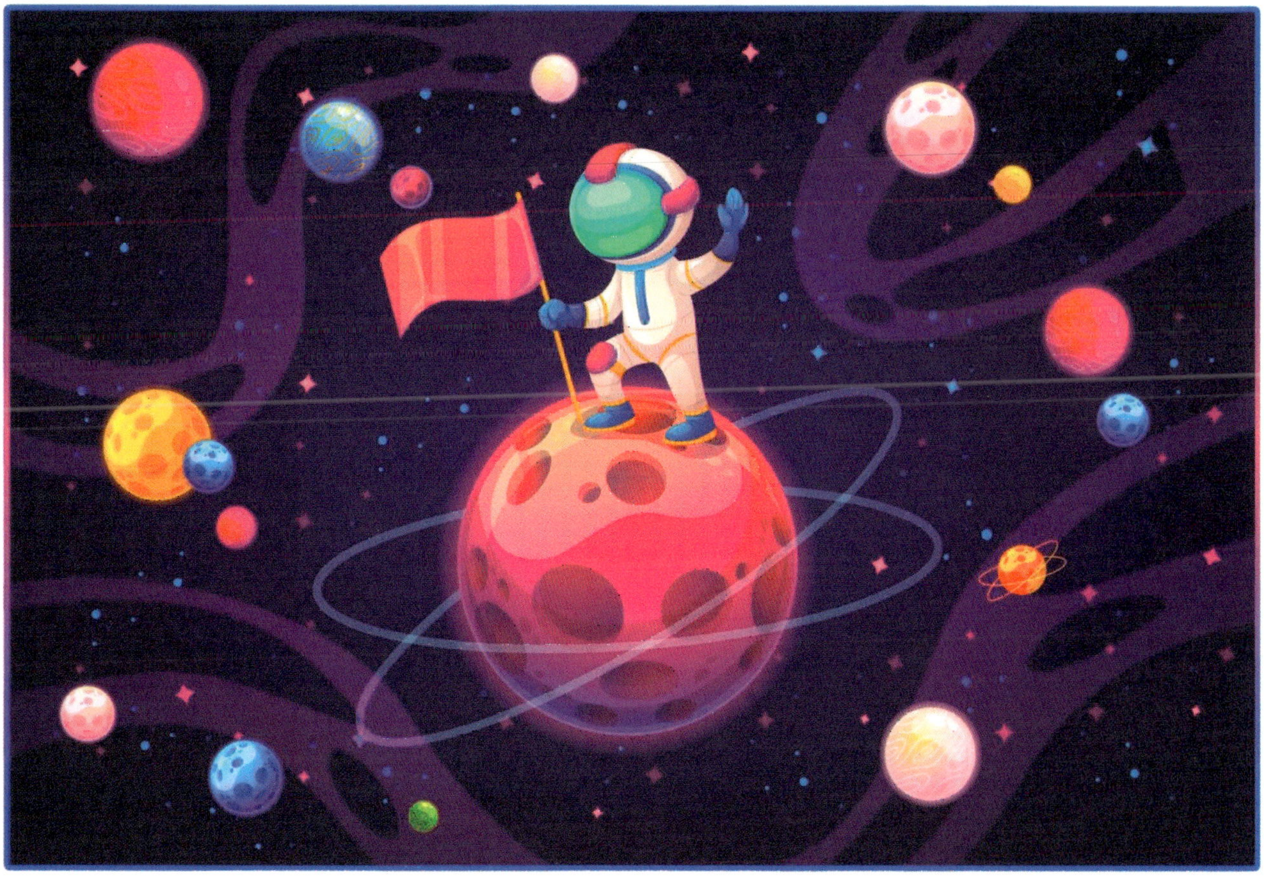

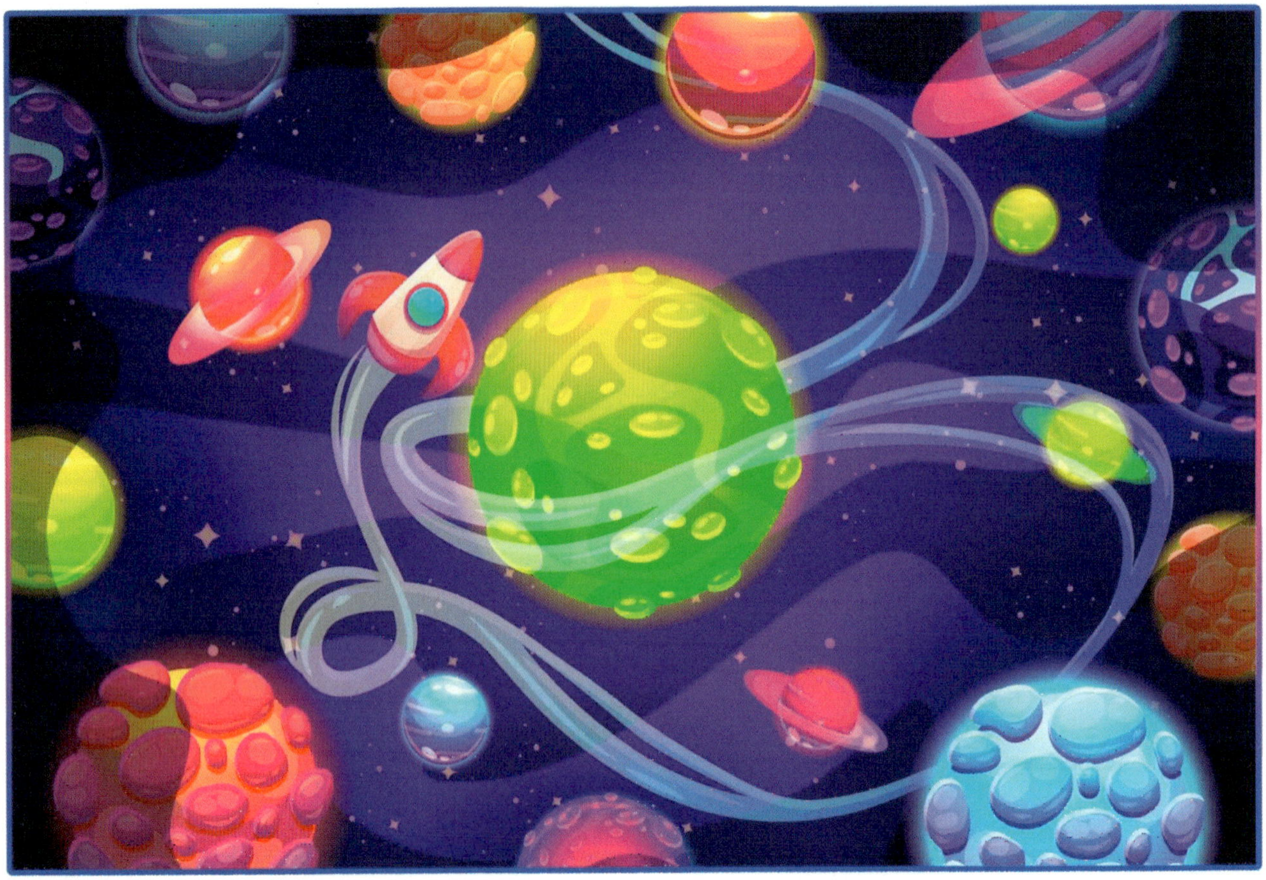
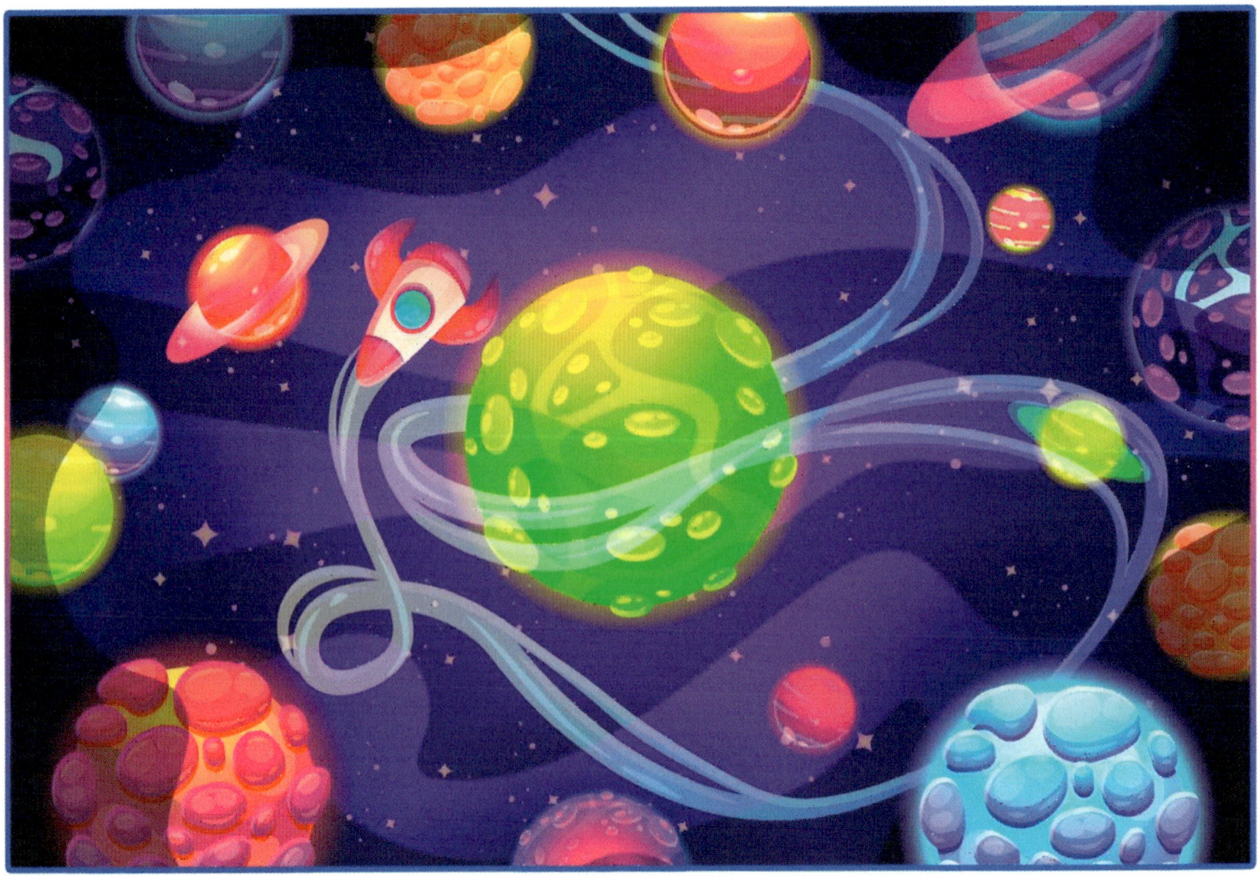

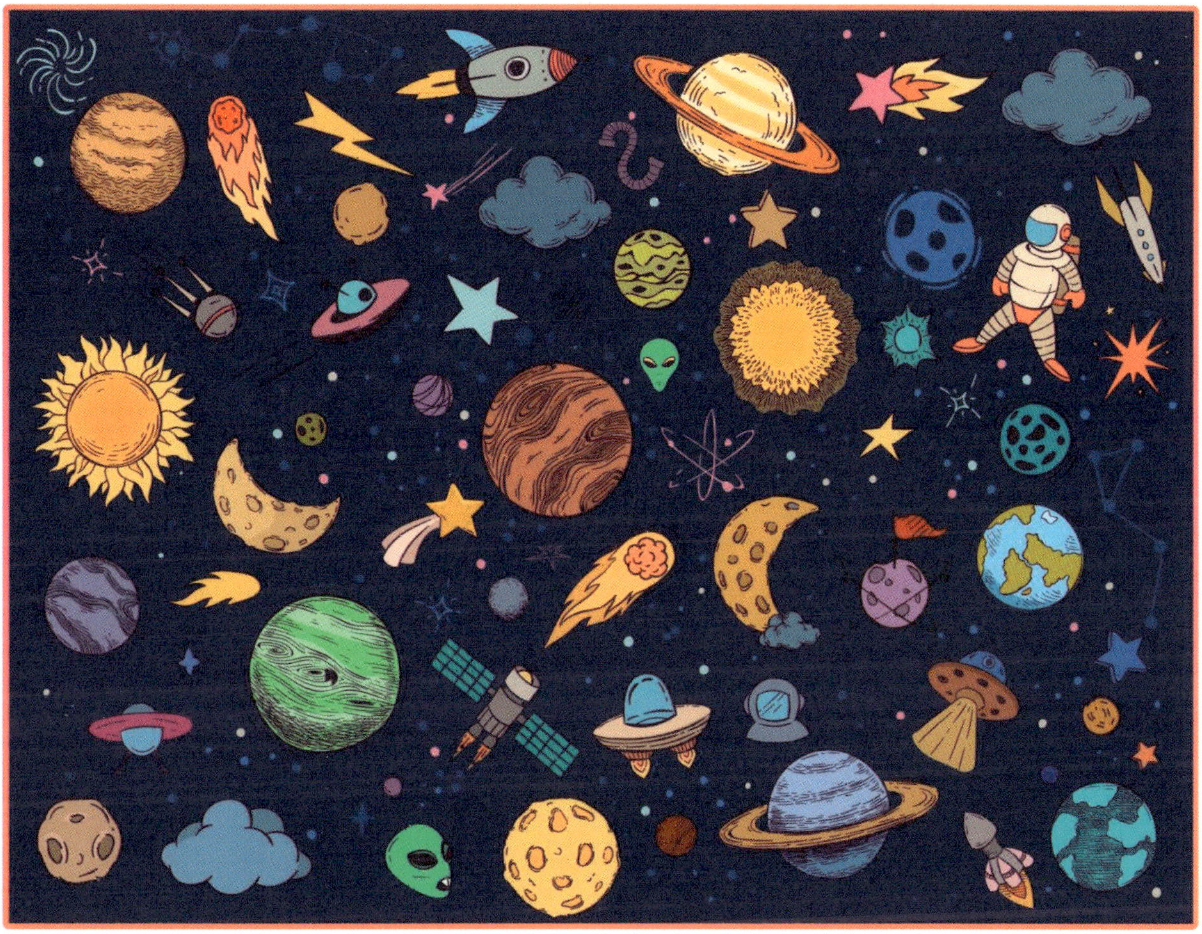

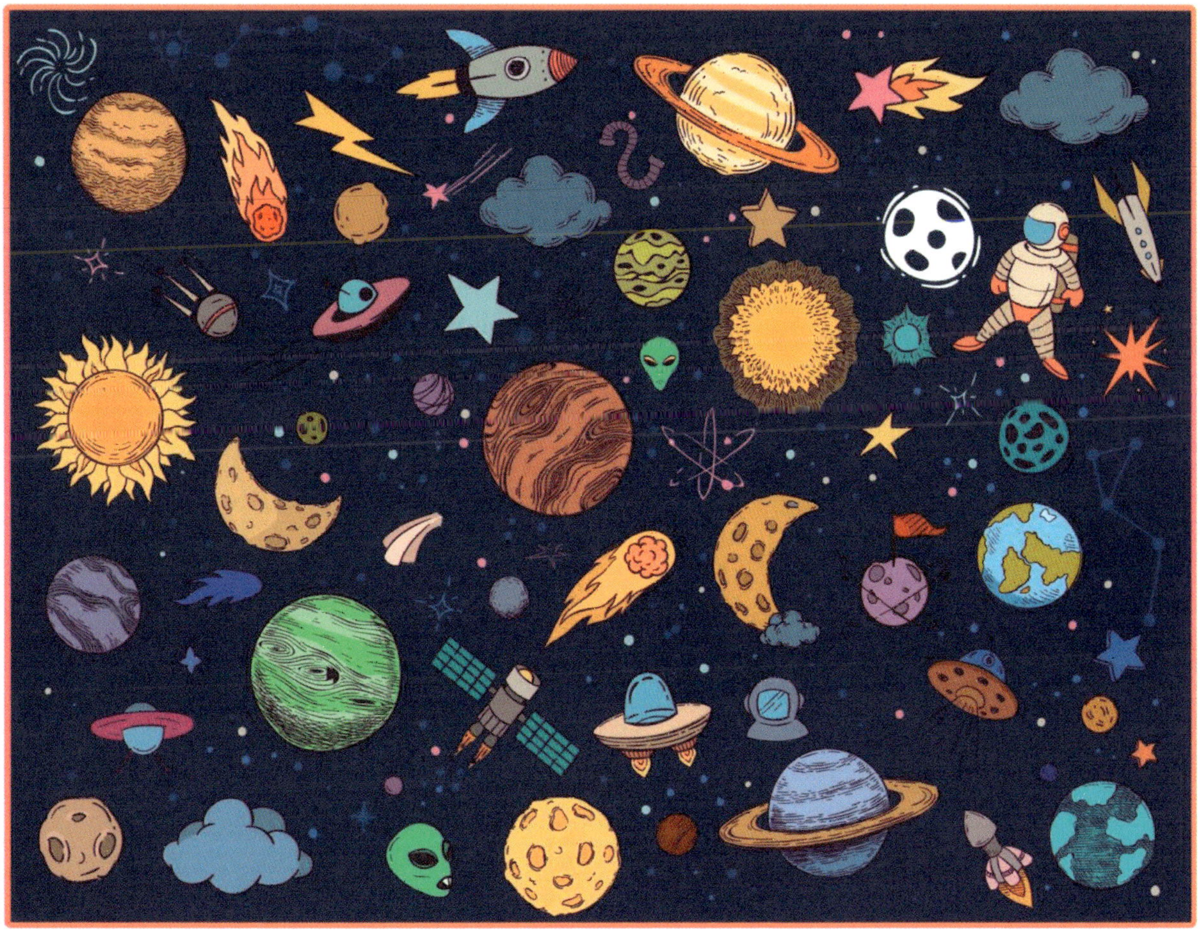

ANSWER

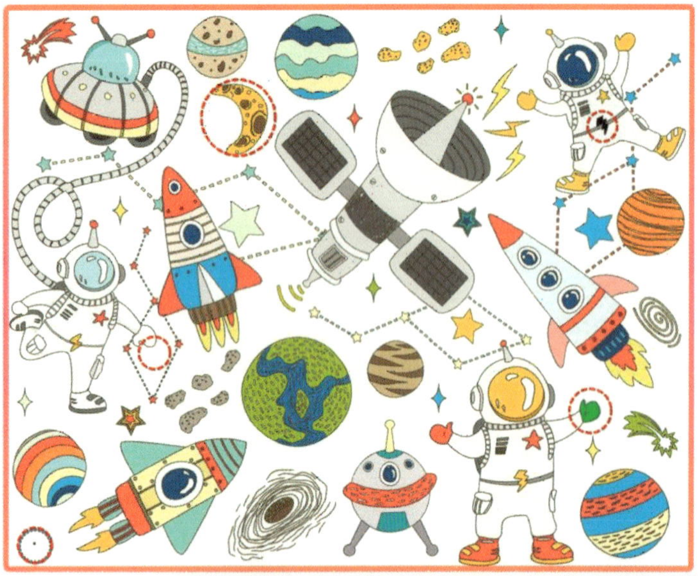

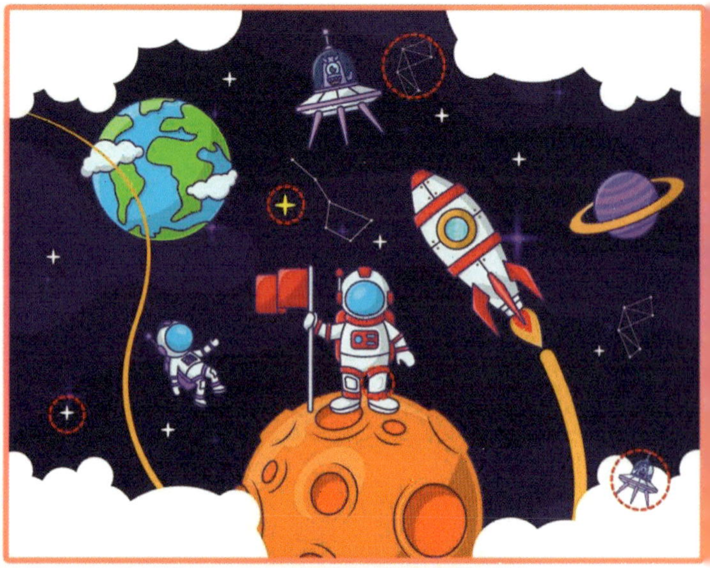

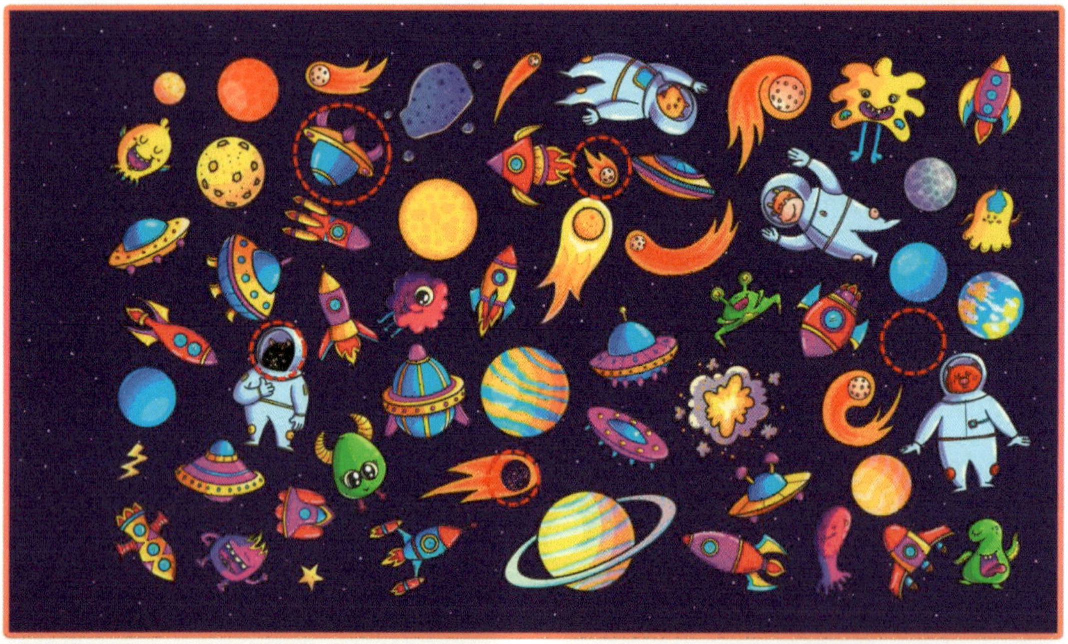

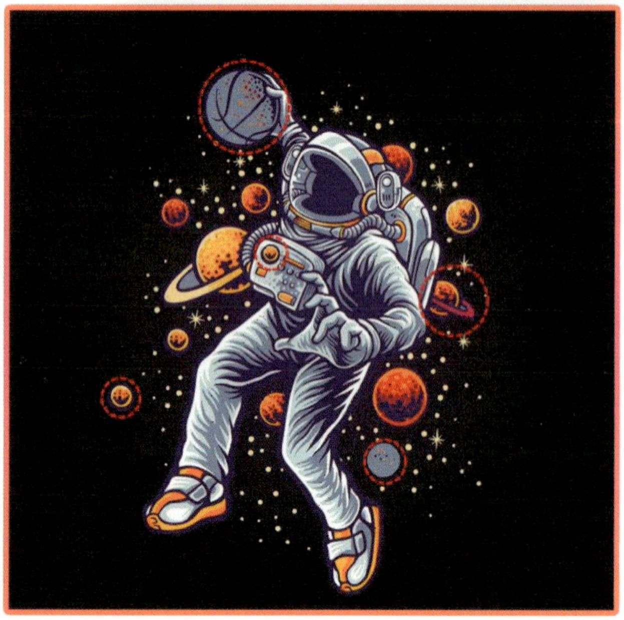

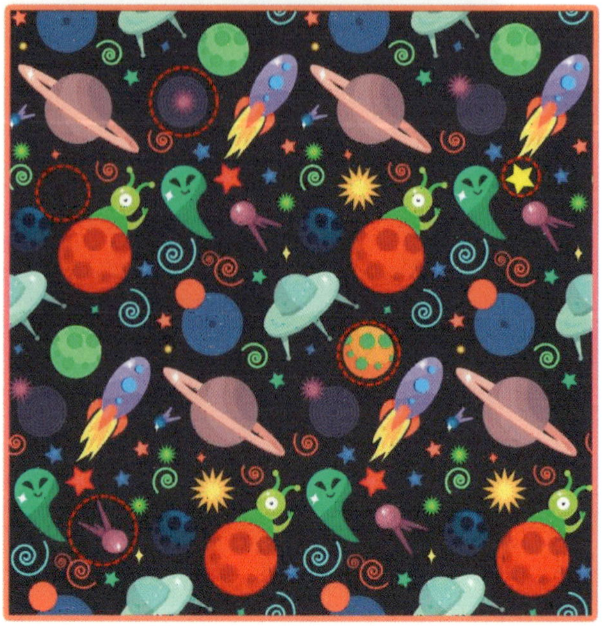

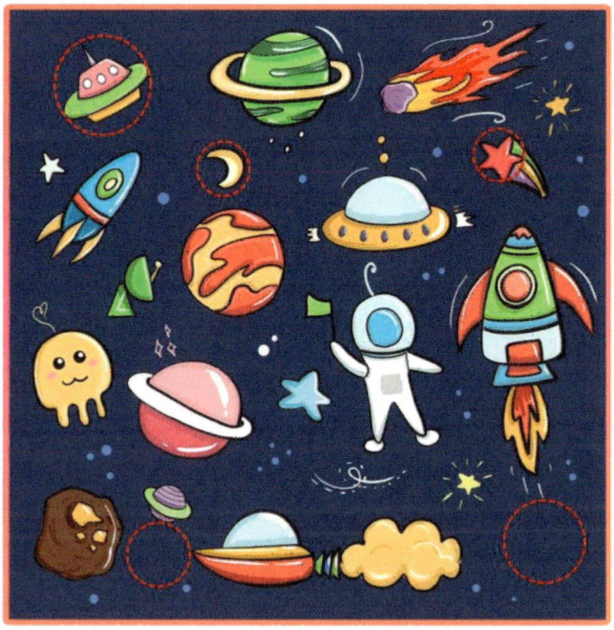
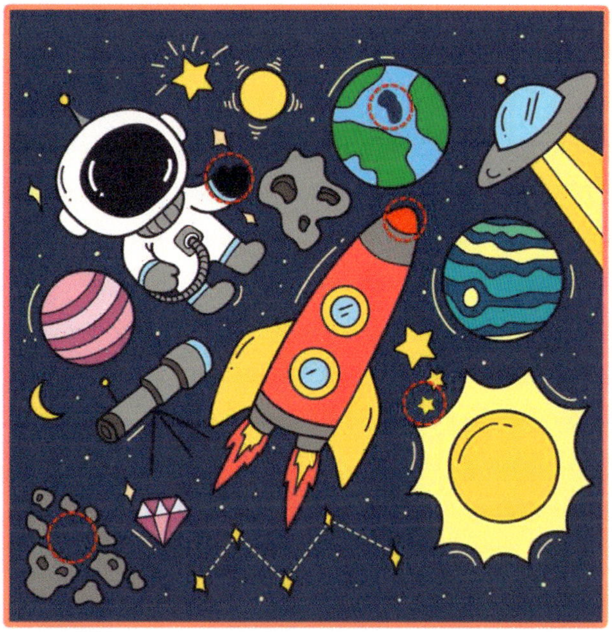
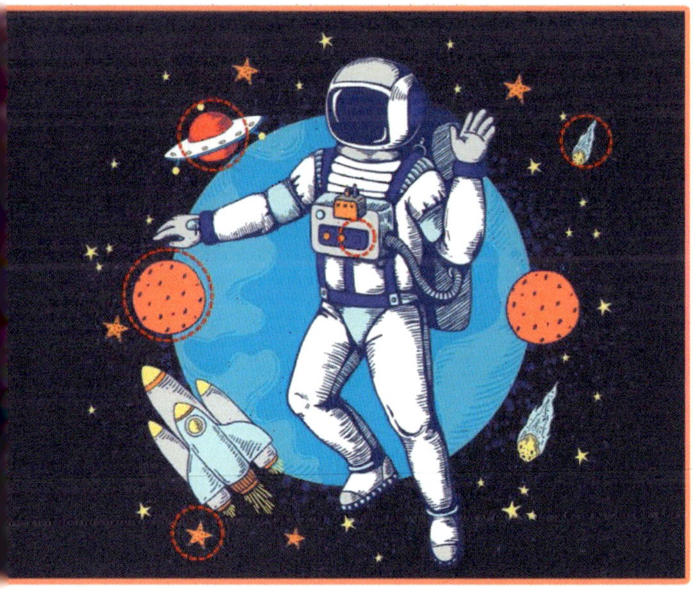
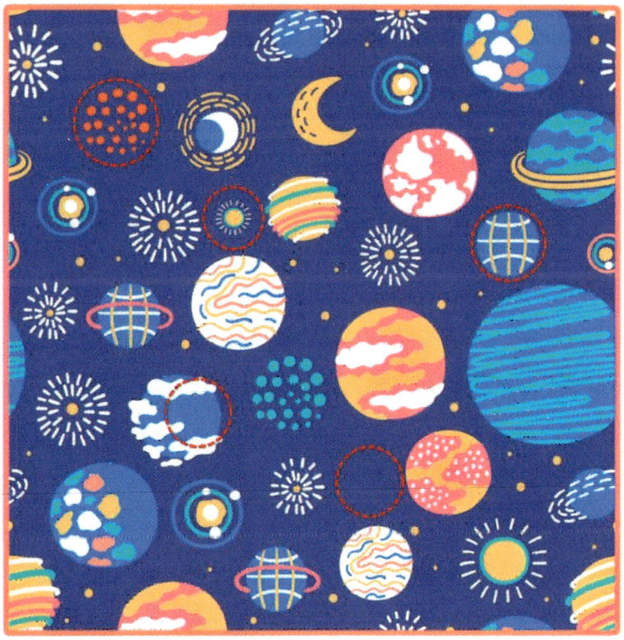
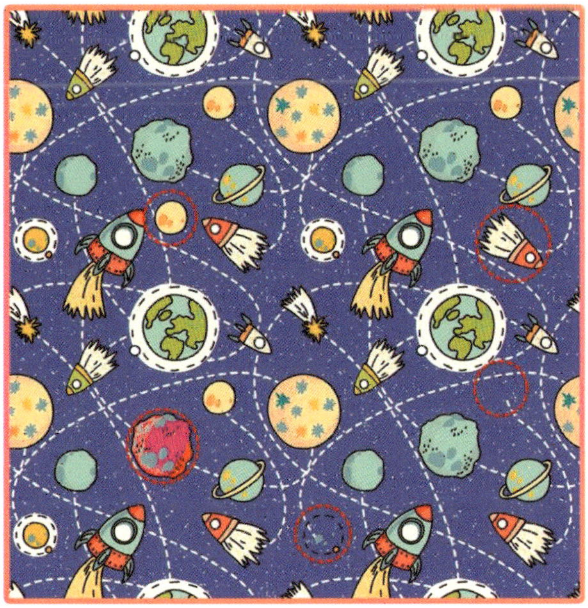

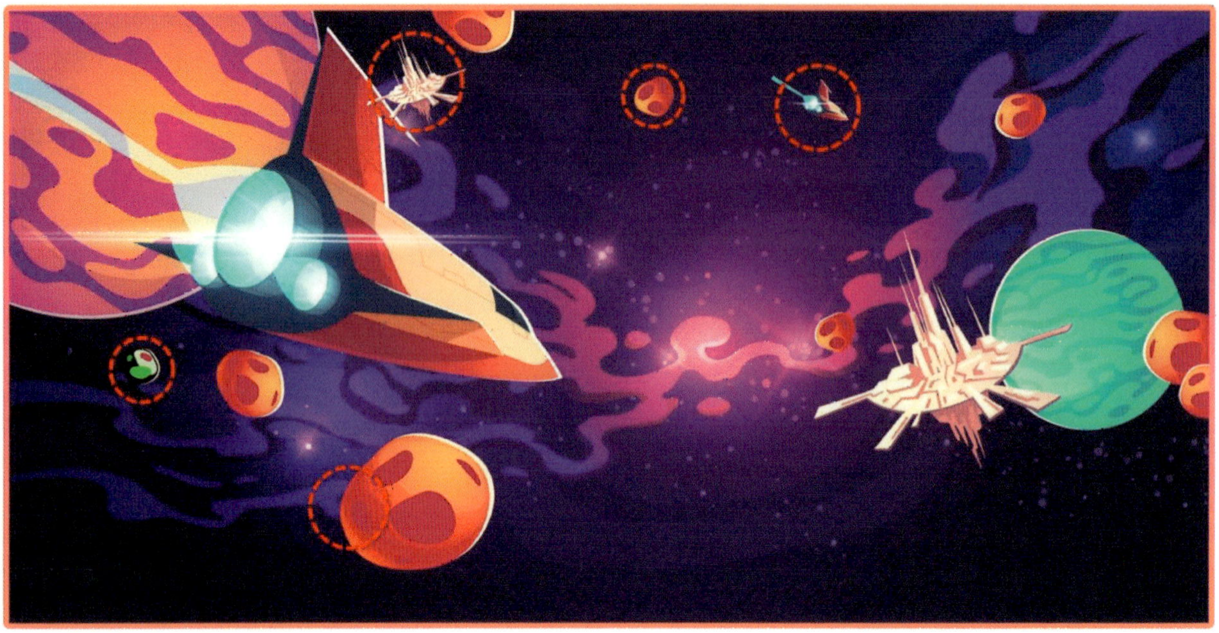

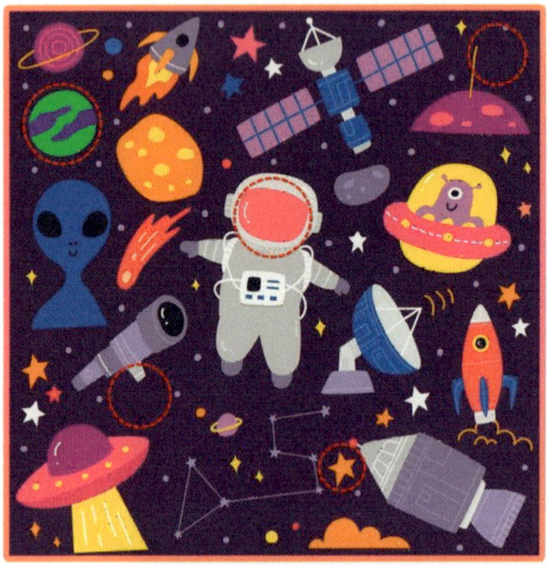

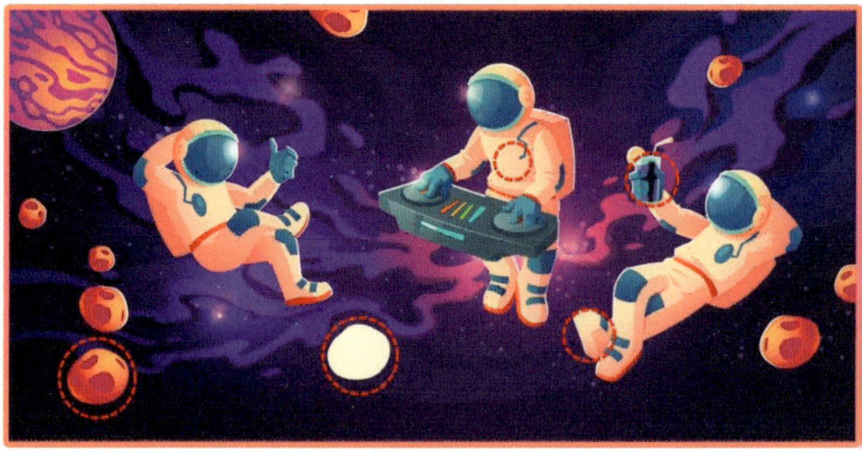

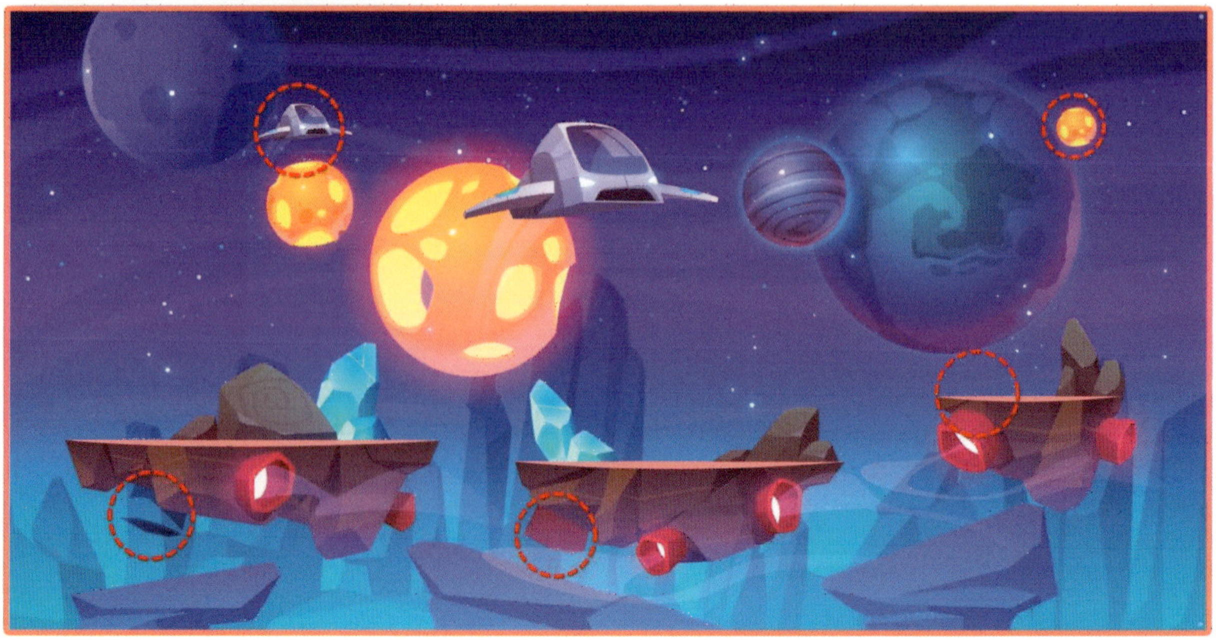

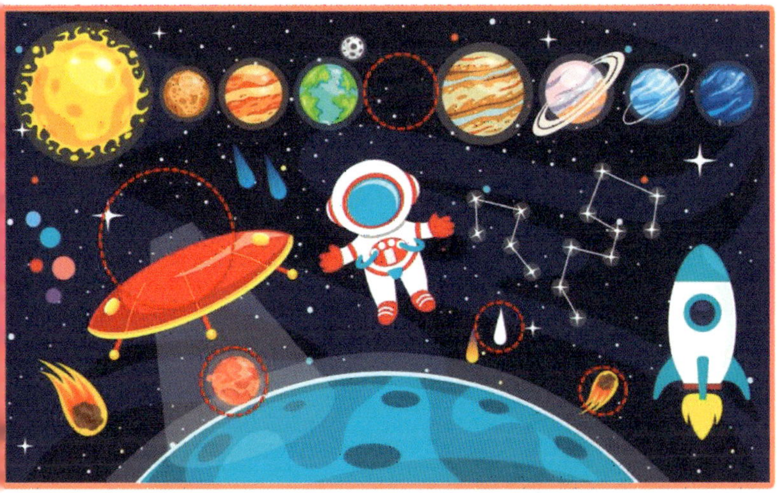

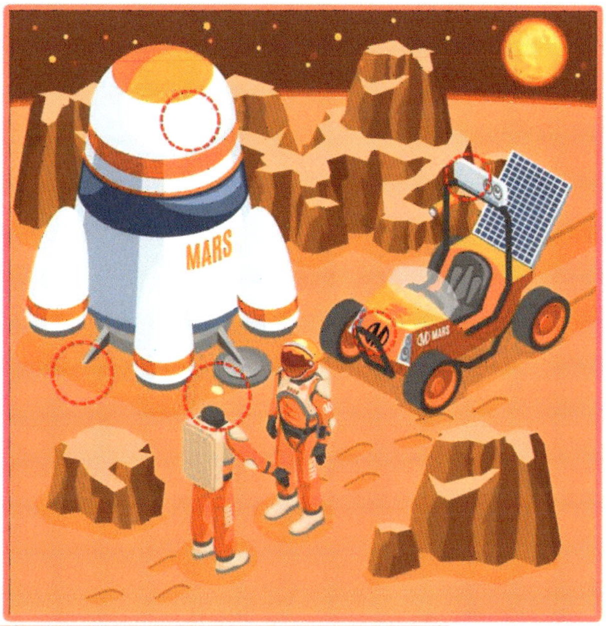
MARS

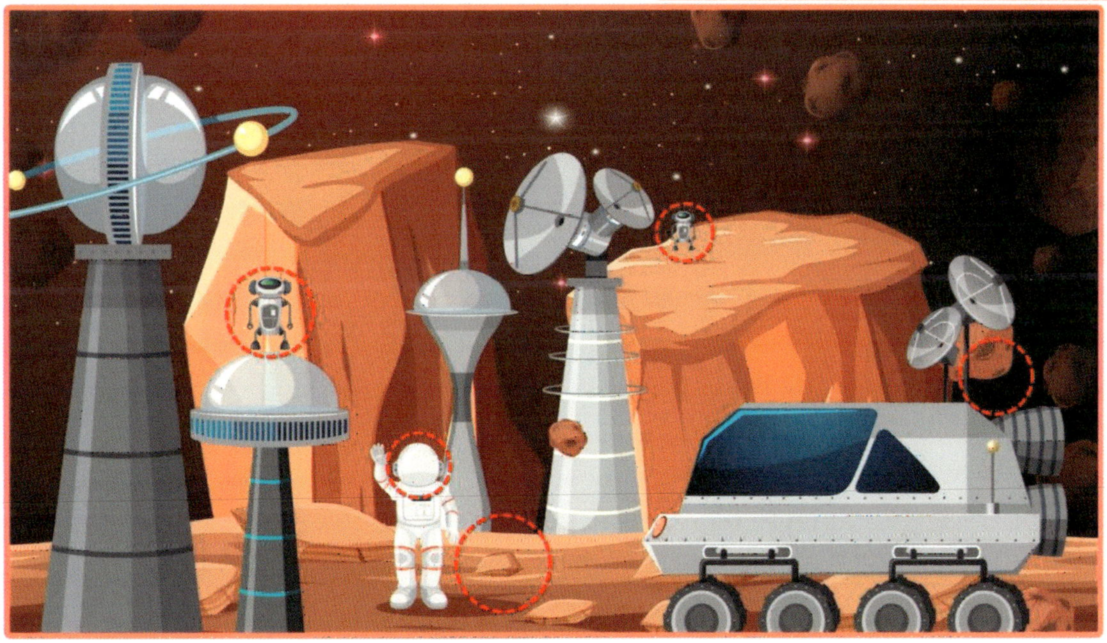

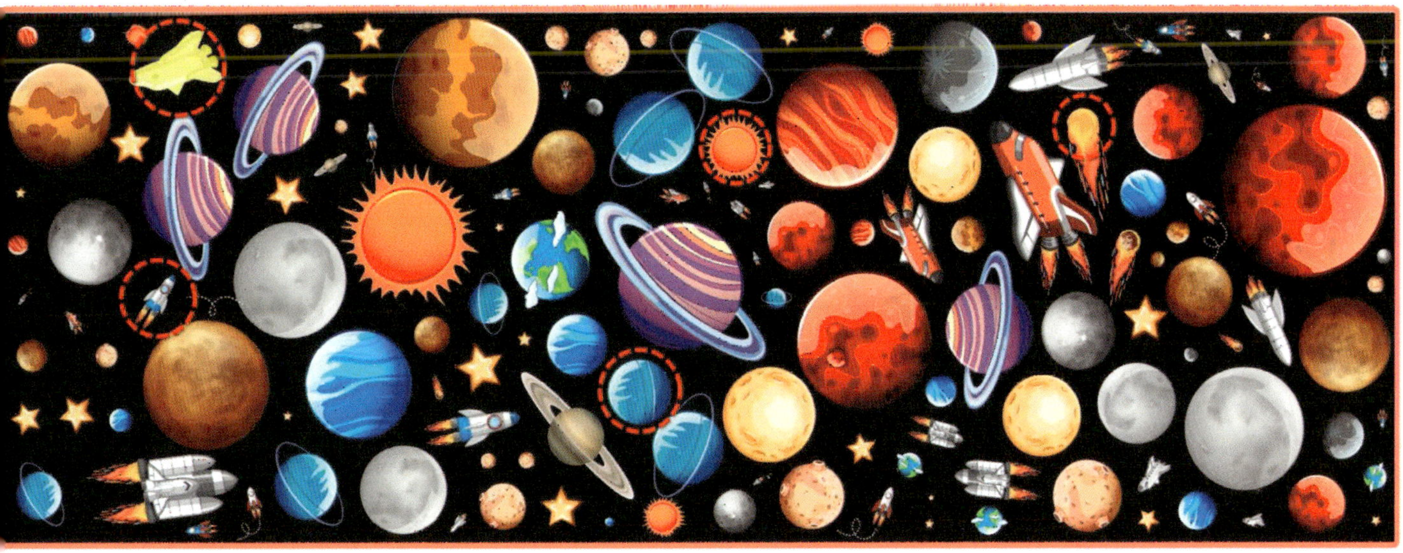

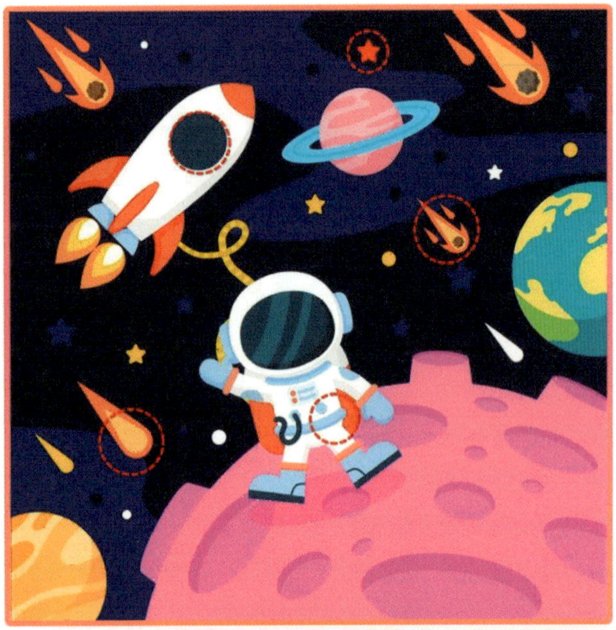

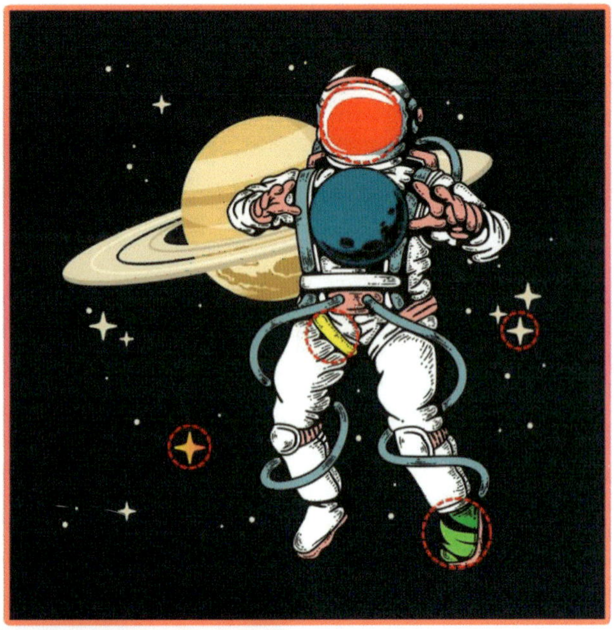

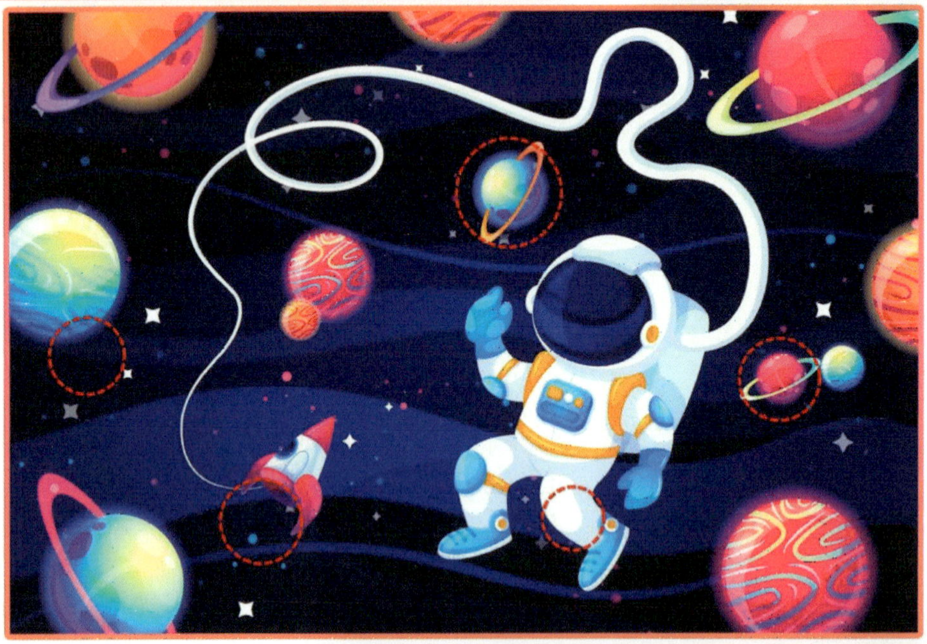

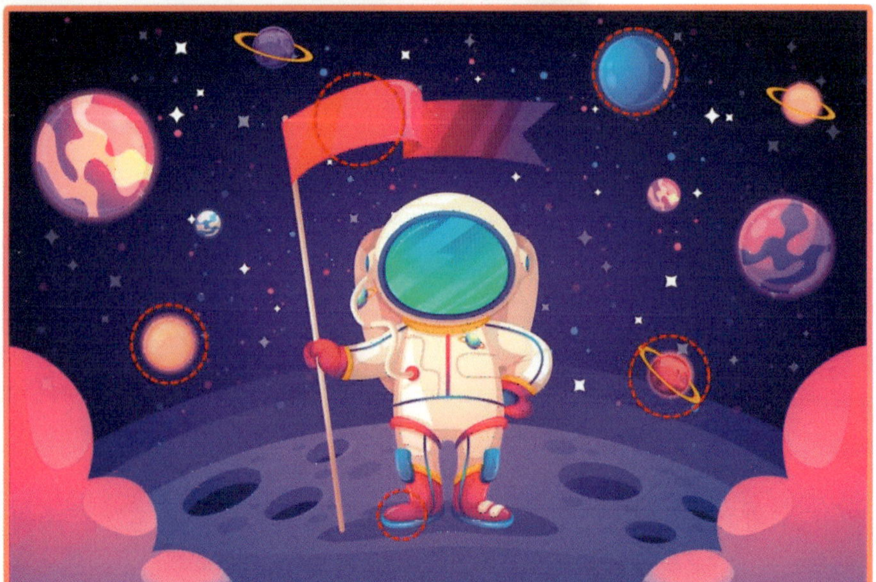

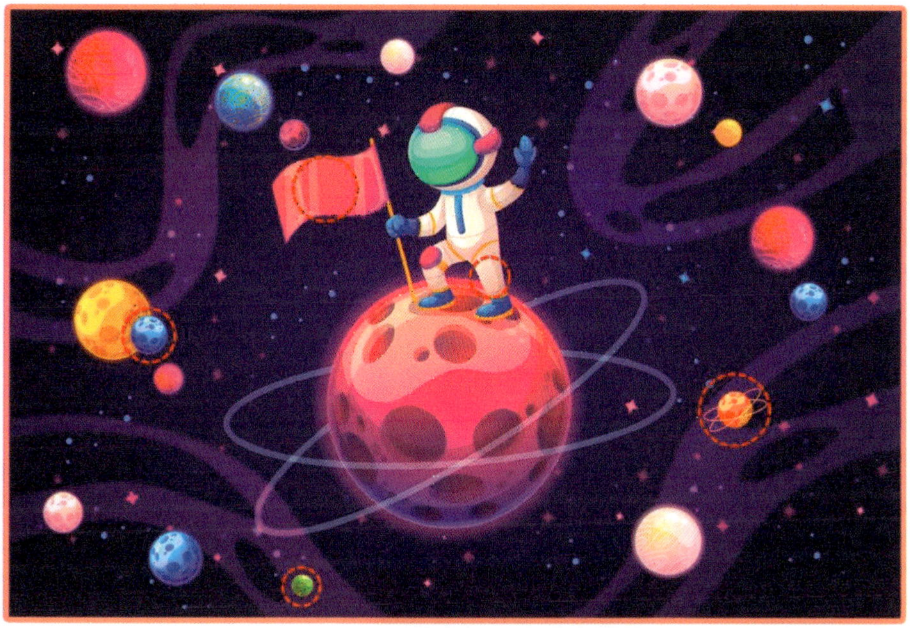

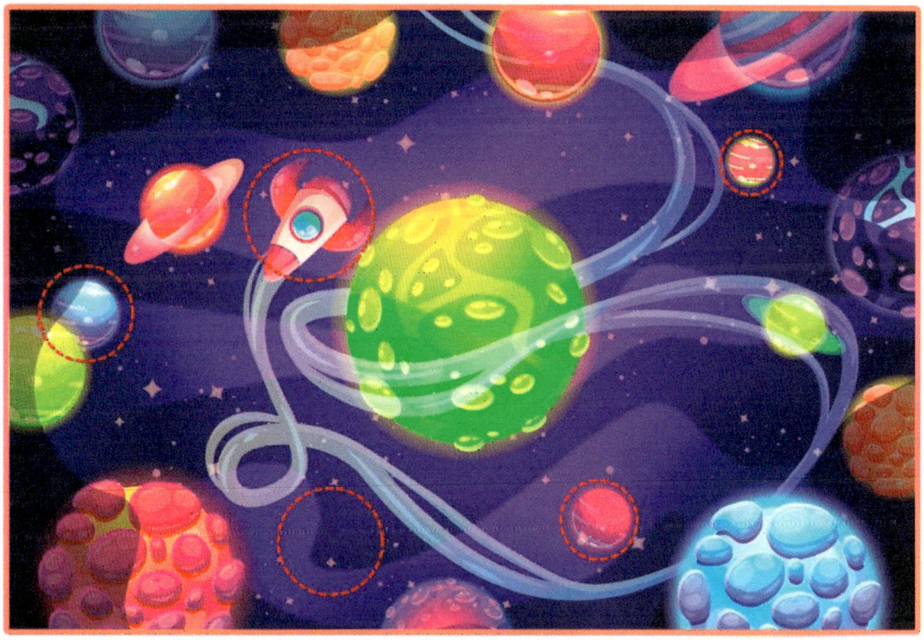

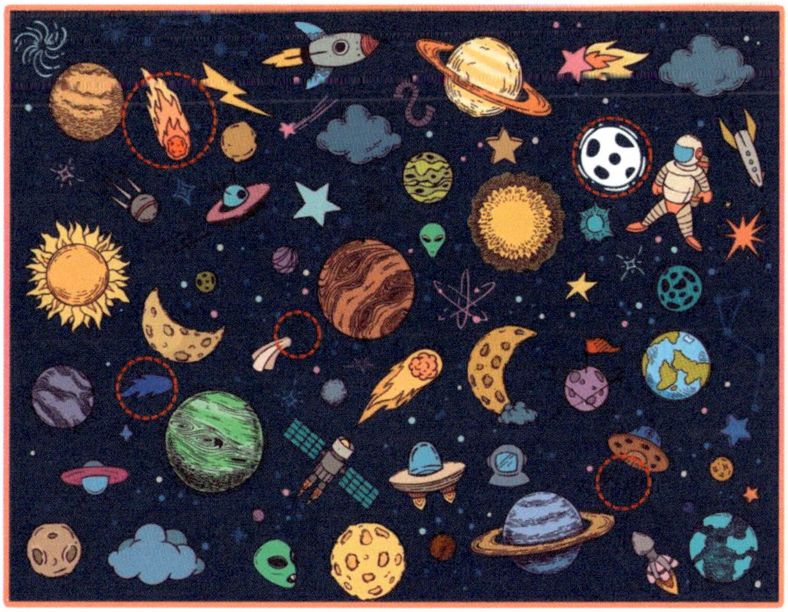

Printed in Great Britain
by Amazon